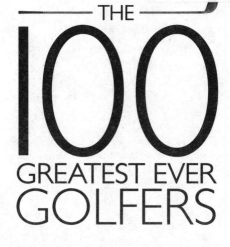

THE 100

GREATEST EVER
GOLFERS

First published 2011 by Elliott and Thompson Limited
27 John Street, London WC1N 2BX
www.eandtbooks.com

ISBN: 978-1-907642-35-7

Foreword © Padraig Harrington 2011
Text © Andy Farrell 2011

Picture credits:
The following photographs are © Charles Briscoe-Knight: Severiano Ballesteros; John Daly; Laura
Davies; David Duval; Ernie Els; Sir Nick Faldo; Raymond Floyd; Sergio Garcia; Retief Goosen; Padraig
Harrington; Juli Inkster; Hale Irwin; Tony Jacklin; Bernhard Langer; Sandy Lyle; Rory McIlroy; Phil
Mickelson; Colin Montgomerie; Jack Nicklaus; Greg Norman; Lorena Ochoa; José María Olazábal;
Se Ri Pak; Nick Price; Vijay Singh; Annika Sörenstam; Karrie Webb; Lee Westwood; Tiger Woods.

The following photographs are © Old Golf Images Archive: Willie Anderson; Tommy Armour;
John Ball; Jim Barnes; Patty Berg; Tommy Bolt; Julius Boros; James Braid; Joe Carr; Billy Casper;
Glenna Collett Vare; Sir Henry Cotton; Jimmy Demaret; George Duncan; Walter Hagen; Harold
Hilton; Ben Hogan; Bobby Jones; Cecil Leitch; Tony Lema; Lawson Little; Bobby Locke; Arnaud
Massy; Cary Middlecoff; Old Tom Morris; Young Tom Morris; Kel Nagle; Byron Nelson; Francis
Ouimet; Arnold Palmer; Willie Park Snr; Gary Player; Betsy Rawls; Ted Ray; Allan Robertson;
Gene Sarazen; Charlie Sifford; Sam Snead; Payne Stewart; Louise Suggs; Freddie Tait; JH Taylor;
Peter Thomson; Jerome Travers; Walter Travis; Lee Trevino; Jessie Valentine; Flory Van Donck;
Harry Vardon; Roberto de Vicenzo; Norman Von Nida; Tom Watson; Joyce Wethered; Mickey
Wright; Babe Zaharias. Please note that while OGI retains the copyright / licence to the vast
majority of its comprehensive archive, it makes every effort to trace the original copyright holder
on any, and all other images it may retain. However in some rare instances this has not always been
possible and we apologise in advance for any omissions that may have inadvertently occurred.
In such cases, should the original copyright holder/photographer/photographic agency contact us
we will, as always, endeavour to credit any such omission.

The following photographs are © Phil Sheldon Picture Library: Isao Aoki; JoAnne Carner;
Bob Charles; Ben Crenshaw; Catherine Lacoste; Nancy Lopez; Johnny Miller; Christy O'Connor
Snr; Curtis Strange; Yani Tseng; Kathy Whitworth; Ian Woosnam.

Sir Michael Bonallack © Getty Images
Darren Clarke © Phil Inglis
Moe Norman and Marlene Stewart Streit © Royal Canadian Golf Association (Golf Canada).

9 8 7 6 5 4 3 2 1

A CIP catalogue record for this book is available from the British Library.

Printed and bound by CPI Group (UK) Ltd, Croydon, CR0 4YY

Designed by James Collins

Every effort has been made to trace copyright holders for extracts
used within this book. Where this has not been possible the publisher
will be happy to credit them in future editions.

THE
100

GREATEST EVER
GOLFERS

ANDY FARRELL

Elliott & Thompson

CONTENTS

THE BIG THREE, 1960–1970

THE NICKLAUS CHALLENGERS, 1970–1980

SEVE AND THE RISE OF EUROPE, 1980–1995

THE TIGER ERA, 1995–2011

FOREWORD

What does it take to be one of the greatest golfers of all time? How do you separate the great from the good? Which is better – the erratic player with the ability to play unbelievably well, or the solid pro without a fifth gear or the ability to up his game? While results will be the predominant factor in determining who are the greatest golfers ever, it is the intricate parts that go together to create an aura around the player, that elevate them into the 'greats' based on flair, ball striking or contribution to the game – those who have brought fans to the sport. It is hard to go along to the practice range and pick out who are the great players based on their ball striking alone, however. Being able to hit the ball well is only part of the equation; being able to compete is even more important. You have to understand the player's drive, their will and desire. You need to understand what separates the men from the boys and sometimes determine which players have achieved so much with less talent.

I have always believed in my old coach, Bob Torrance's mantra: 'A good player can play great when the feeling is upon him but a great player can play good when he wants to.' As you will read from the selection of the 100 greatest ever golfers, some players are selected based on the fact that they had the ability to play great every so often rather than have it on demand. To get there, the great players have to put in many hours, days, weeks and months on the practice range. Many of them put in a huge amount of work even before they came to the tour, but this is not necessarily the case for all – there are no set rules and there are different ways of becoming a great player. You would be very naive to believe that Tiger's talents were given to him; he earned every bit of his game on the range and on the golf course and ultimately it had more to do with his drive and his want than any physical gift. Yet someone like Colin Montgomerie practised relatively little but trusted what he had, allowing him to be fresh come Sunday afternoon and go on to win many tournaments.

There is no better feeling than the satisfaction that comes with knowing a job has been well done. Personally, the highs of winning three major championships will stay with me my whole life, but Bob's quote above has meant that I have spent more time searching for the magical secret which keeps it fun and drives me on. It is all too easy to put other brilliant players on a pedestal – while the likes of Ernie Els, Retief Goosen and Tiger were winning majors, it was hard to see myself matching them. However, I know Michael Campbell very well. Having played with him many times, I knew his game and his ability, and after he won the US Open in 2005 it was easier to visualise myself winning a major. The European golfers now winning majors, or who might win majors, have seen me play golf. They have seen me hit good shots and they have seen me hit bad shots. They understand my game, the way I've played, how hard I've worked. As a result, they are less likely to think they are so far away.

I think there are two main reasons why European golf is strong at the moment. The first is that we had such great role models and grew up watching Seve, Faldo, Langer, Lyle and Woosie, as well as other non-Americans like Greg Norman and Nick Price, dominate the world of golf. As a kid I thought it was normal for the international players to win majors. It may have been the first time for many decades that the best players in the world were not just from America, but as a child I didn't realise that.

Secondly, on the European Tour there is nowhere to hide. It gives you a lot of opportunities to get into contention – and you only really learn about your game and yourself when a tournament is on the line – but you are also required to perform week-in, week-out. If you are one of the marquee players at a tournament, there is a giant poster of you by the entrance and people are expecting you to deliver. If you don't perform, everyone – all the sponsors, the press, the people running the tournament – want to know, 'What went wrong?' In the States it can be a lot easier – you miss the cut and you are gone, with no one to trouble you.

Trying to come up with the 100 greatest ever golfers is an intriguing exercise. You, like me, may not agree with all the inclusions in the book but it is fun to debate and everyone's opinion is interesting. The more I started thinking about it, the more I kept changing my mind. I know one player has already caused a lot of debate but I would go along with Rory McIlroy's inclusion. While we all might agree that he will probably end up among the greats, is he one now? I would say 'yes' and for this reason: he may have only won one major (and that might not qualify him) and he's only won a couple of other tour events (which also might not qualify him), but he's won a major by eight strokes, and there are only a handful of players who have ever done that. For his sheer brilliance and amazing scoring at Congressional in the 2011 US Open, I would certainly include him.

If nothing else, Rory already makes for a great story and I believe all the fascinating accounts of the great players in this book make for a terrific read. Who is the greatest of them all? Personally I would go for the cliché, Jack Nicklaus. He was a strong golfer and even better mentally. I admire and aspire to the second trait so, for me, it's Jack – no question.

Padraig Harrington
2011

INTRODUCTION

I n the mid-19th century it was a truth universally acknowledged, at least in golf, which at the time meant St. Andrews, other spots on the east coast of Scotland and the odd outpost like Prestwick, that Allan Robertson was the greatest of golfers. He was a highly regarded maker of clubs and balls, he was a caddie, and when he played, he rarely lost. At foursomes in combination with his apprentice, Tom Morris, the two men were said to be unbeatable.

'It was an article of faith with many old golfers that Allan Robertson was the best player that had ever handled a club,' wrote Horace Hutchinson, golfing historian and a fine player himself in the late 19th century. Donald Steel and Peter Ryde in the *Shell International Encyclopedia of Golf* stated: 'He was by common consent the supreme golfer of his age.'

A book like this one would have been a lot shorter if published in the age of Robertson. At least the selection process would have been a lot less difficult. So much has happened in golf in the century and a half since, that the problem now is the opposite. Not whom to include, but whom to leave out?

To identify the 100 greatest ever golfers was a tempting but dangerous proposal. The project was like the best of courses, one that is never less than a pleasure to play but one which never fails to ensnare the player in its labyrinthine subtleties. Everyone can agree on the legends – Vardon, Jones, Hogan, Nicklaus, Palmer, Seve and Woods. And plenty of other greats – Young Tom Morris, JH Taylor and James

Braid, Walter Hagen and Gene Sarazen, Byron Nelson, Sam Snead, Peter Thomson, Gary Player, Lee Trevino, Tom Watson, Nick Faldo, Joyce Wethered and Mickey Wright. Perhaps half, or even two-thirds, pick themselves. Of course, the interesting bit is settling on the last few names. Why pick them as opposed to the dozens left out? Two issues soon became apparent. The first was not being able to agree with myself from one day to the next. It should be made clear from the outset that there were no fixed criteria for inclusion in this book. No manufactured points table, nor recalculated money lists taking into account inflation and the like. Golfing greatness can only ever exist in the eye of the beholder. My opinions have been formed over two decades as a golf writer. But the more I read while researching this book, and the more I talked to other people, so further contemplation always seemed essential in order to refine the 'List'.

The other consideration was that events kept occurring during the writing of the book – weekly, in terms of the tours, although these had only a minor effect on my thinking; and, more occasionally, the major championships of 2011, which always had a significant bearing on the List, even if the winner did not eventually make the cut, so to speak.

There is a reason for this. Over the last 150 or so years, championship golf has proved itself remarkably proficient in identifying the greatest players of the game. Although there have always been matches and exhibitions, tournaments and tours, there have always been titles that have been the most sought after. Over time, however, the players who prevail most often in the championships where everyone who's anyone gets to tee-up, and the ones who most often win the oldest and most treasured trophies, are the greatest players.

Robertson, of course, never won what we know today as a major championship. They did not exist in his lifetime. There was no need of them. His death, however, may well have helped introduce the concept of championship golf. As the *Shell Encyclopedia* records: 'He died the year before the first Open Championship so that his name is not entered on the roll of honour, but it is said that the championship arose out of a desire to find out who ruled the roost once the matter had been thrown into doubt by Robertson's death.'

For the previous few years, the idea of a championship had been proposed by the Earl of Eglinton and Colonel James Ogilvie Fairlie, two bigwigs at Prestwick. They had already shown they were forward thinkers by persuading Old Tom Morris to leave St. Andrews and develop a new links on the west coast. Perhaps Robertson's death in 1859 concentrated various minds, and so on October 17, 1860, at Prestwick, eight players made three loops of the 12-hole course and Willie Park was the champion. All the players were caddies, and hence professionals, so it was not very open at all. However, amateurs were eligible for the Open from the following year.

After a quarter of a century, in which time no amateur had managed to win the Open, the Amateur Championship, which excluded professionals, was created in 1885. It was not long however before two British amateurs, John Ball and Harold Hilton, beat the professionals to win the Open. In 1895, the United States Golf Association conducted the first US Open and the first US Amateur Championship. There now existed a quartet of titles representing the pinnacles of the game, and Bobby Jones wanted to win them all – in the same year.

It was 1930 and Jones achieved exactly what he set out to do, winning the British Amateur, for the first and only time, at St. Andrews, then the Open at Hoylake, the US Open at Interlachen and finally the US Amateur at Merion. He was 28 and had no more golfing Everests to climb. He retired.

Thirty years later Arnold Palmer was trying to come up with a professional golfer's modern equivalent of Jones's Grand Slam – the term 'Impregnable Quadrilateral', though a magnificent phrase, never quite caught on. He had won the Masters, which Jones had founded at his own golf course of Augusta National in 1934, and the US Open, and was flying to Britain alongside his friend and golf writer Bob Drum. They thought that, if Palmer could win the Open and then return home and claim the USPGA Championship, first organised by the PGA of America in 1916, then he too could claim a Grand Slam. Ben Hogan had won the Masters and the US Open in 1953 and went on to win the Open at Carnoustie, his only attempt at the claret jug. Because of a car accident a few years earlier, he no longer played in the physically more demanding USPGA with its matchplay format of 36 holes a day.

Palmer came up just short at the 1960 Open at St. Andrews but though his quest for a Grand Slam was stymied, his subsequent return to the 'British', and double triumph in the following two years, undoubtedly helped make the Open the ultimate championship it is today. However, America's domination of the sport for most of the 20th century is the reason why three of the four majors are in the States. Fast forward to 2000 when Tiger Woods won the US Open, the Open and the USPGA before going on to claim the 2001 Masters. With all four trophies sitting on his coffee table, Woods was not concerned with the pedants' arguments about whether his Tiger Slam measured up to a calendar-year Grand Slam. In truth, winning all four of the modern majors over a lifetime, let alone within 12 months, is hard enough – and has only been achieved so far by Gene Sarazen, Ben Hogan, Jack Nicklaus, Gary Player and Woods.

So championship golf provides us with a framework for revealing greatness, but a player's achievements are only half of the ledger. Greatness is not just about what someone does, it is also about how we, the observers, feel about it and how it inspires us. There can be no set formula for greatness, no list of qualifications – we just know it when we see it. So if winning the big championships, the ones that mean the most to the players – men or women, amateur or professional, ancient or modern – is the primary criterion for judging greatness, it cannot be the only one. If it were, the list of multiple major winners would suffice as an index of greatness.

Instead, we must take other factors into account. Popularity is an important one because it corresponds directly to how we feel about a player. In golf, spectators vote with their feet, pounding the fairways alongside their favourites – so Freddie Tait and Joe Carr must be considered alongside other adventurous golfers such as Young Tom Morris, Arnold Palmer and Seve Ballesteros. Have there been two more loved women golfers than Nancy Lopez and Lorena Ochoa?

Then there are those who have been pioneers for the game around the globe, such as Flory Van Donck in Europe, Norman Von Nida in Australia, Argentina's Roberto de Vicenzo, Japan's Isao Aoki and Se Ri Pak from South Korea. Marlene Stewart Streit dominated the amateur game in Canada but also won the most prestigious titles in America and Britain. Moe Norman hardly won anything outside Canada and gave up on the American circuit for social rather than golfing reasons. His is a fascinating story. Norman's appearances on the practice range at the Canadian Open late in his life had the modern professionals queuing up to catch a glimpse of the legend's swing.

Some players touch greatness in spite of their own worst faults, like Tommy 'Thunder' Bolt, or did so amid a tumultuous life, like John Daly. Colin Montgomerie, Sergio Garcia and Lee Westwood have yet to win a major but Monty won a record seven European order of merits in a row, Garcia won the Players Championship, the so-called 'fifth major', and Westwood has been world number one. All are Ryder Cup heroes and had to be considered alongside the major winners.

But what does it take to be a great player? If there are no absolute criteria, are there at least common traits that we can recognise? What separates the great player from the merely very good? A lifelong commitment to the game is a basic foundation for any good player. But a great player takes full advantage of his or her opportunities, perhaps to the extent that a good player cannot imagine.

Malcolm Gladwell's book *Outliers* makes clear that a happy accident of circumstance can give someone exposure to a skill for far longer than most other people. So look out for the number of great players who grew up on a golf course, next to a golf course or worked as a caddie as a youngster. Think of Francis Ouimet gazing out of his bedroom window at the glory that is the Country Club of Brookline, and sneaking on at dawn before anyone else was about. Seve Ballesteros also had to play the odd hole at Pedreña when no one was looking, and otherwise spent his time on the beach hitting his old three-iron. Top-notch facilities are not required. Byron Nelson claimed the unkempt, sun-baked, wind-swept courses of Texas in the Great Depression were perfect for developing talent and especially the ability to adapt to any circumstance.

However, just having time – and, as Gladwell tells us, 10,000 hours or ten years is now the accepted standard for developing an expertise in a skill ('I spent that just warming up with each club,' joked Sir Nick Faldo) – is not enough. As Matthew Syed demonstrates in *Bounce: How Champions are Made*, purposeful practice is required to keep developing an expertise. Ben Hogan illustrated this beautifully. As a journeyman, Hogan's scattergun approach to practising did not help him. When he worked religiously on a few fundamentals, he became the best player of his generation.

Faldo's development was aided by imagination and visualisation. He pretended to play as other players, Nicklaus, Palmer, Player, Miller, even Hogan or Snead, whom he had never seen in person. It was a form of visualisation which allowed Faldo to gain confidence from the good shots and assign any bad shots to whomever he was impersonating. His other trick was to treat his home club of Welwyn Garden City as a template for more challenging holes by imagining a water hazard or out-of-bounds line. But the most fun was simply hitting, say, a seven-iron all day. 'By the end of the day the club was just an extension of your arm,' Faldo explained. 'Jeepers, talk about being about to feel the cover of the ball. You were so confident.' So what a good player might think of as hard work, a great player thinks of as fun.

Obviously, commitment, dedication and perseverance are all required. Golfers, even the greatest, spend more time losing than winning. For many, it is through losing that they learn how to win. Padraig Harrington could be considered a slow learner. He has been a runner-up numerous times (29 at the time of writing) but when his chance came, he was ready, winning three majors in two years. 'Winning is a good habit but you don't learn much,' he said. 'You learn a lot when you lose. Sitting in your hotel room at 10 o'clock at night when you have thrown away a tournament is not a nice experience, going over what you did wrong in your head.' It was Harrington who told Rory McIlroy that the young man was a better player the Monday after the 2011 Masters, than the Monday before. A horrifying collapse in the final round might have defined McIlroy's young career, except he rewrote the script at the US Open.

Amnesia can be a useful quality for the great player to have. Jack Nicklaus simply never remembered when he lost – and he had more seconds and thirds in majors than anyone. But he never forgot how to win. When he was charging to victory at the 1986 Masters, Tom Weiskopf, who won the Open but was a runner-up four times at Augusta, was asked on television what Nicklaus was thinking. 'If I knew that,' Weiskopf replied, 'I would have won this tournament.'

Was Nicklaus thinking anything? He did not have to think about 'taking one shot at a time' because it came naturally to him. His utter absorption in the task at hand was the very definition of mindfulness. He said that in major championships he could keep playing his game longer than others could play theirs. Bobby Jones meant something similar when he said: 'Competitive golf, especially strokeplay, demands that the player be continually on the lookout against himself.' It is easier said than done. As the coach Denis Pugh puts it: 'The players that are merely very good, try to play great golf, some imaginary, perfect game. But the players that are great just keep trying to play very good golf. That's the difference.'

But Faldo also pointed out the ability of champions to raise their game when the moment requires it:

> The great ones can make things happen. You have another gear. It used to be fifth, it's now probably a sixth. When you need to turn it on, it inspires you to play better. Bjorn Borg was my first sporting hero, Ayrton Senna, people like that. Anybody who can make their tools sing for them is pretty inspiring.

Standards of play may be rising all the time with improvements in course conditions, equipment, coaching and swing analysis. But better technical skills are not enough if you cannot make use of them. 'Target practice is all well and good, and you might have a badge to say that you are a good marksman but that doesn't necessarily mean you'll be a good guerrilla fighter,' said Peter Thomson. 'You have to have the ability to compete, to survive, not to let the fear of success overwhelm you.'

Thomson also said: 'The super players have one vital quality: calmness.' He and Nicklaus were the prime examples. Calmness and the ability never to give up are the ingredients that help a great player separate themselves from other players with similar technical skills. 'The mental fortitude you have to have to win, the nerves, the skill, it has always been the same,' said Ken Brown, the former Ryder Cup player.

'Look at Gary Player,' said David Leadbetter, the coach. 'What did he have over everyone else? Here and here,' pointing at his heart and his head. 'It's that inner belief that is the intangible that separates the great from the really good.'

That inner belief drives an unshakeable will to win. For Tiger Woods, it is that simple. 'The biggest thing is to have the mindset and the belief you can win every tournament going in,' he said. 'A lot of guys don't have that; Nicklaus had it. He felt he was going to beat everybody.' Nicklaus himself said: 'You have to be strong enough and tough enough and selfish enough to say, "I've got to do this for myself. I've got to get this done for me."'

Betsy Rawls, one of the early LPGA stars, felt that great players have a:

> ... tremendous drive to win and a need to prove themselves to the world. There is a great confidence in one area and a great need in the other to prove you are a worthwhile person. You have the feeling inside that you're very worthwhile, but you need everyone else to know it. Winners take that avenue to prove to the world they are worthwhile, and they can do it through golf. I had a lot of drive and any great player must have an obsession with winning and a need to win.

Another of the great American women players was Patty Berg, who made a list about the qualities she felt were required to be a winner, as recorded by Liz Kahn in *The LPGA: The History of the Ladies Professional Golf Association*. It is worth reproducing not as some self-help mantra but as an example of how differently great players think, how the positive attitude cannot be reinforced enough, and how the repetition is fundamental to the message:

1. Believe you have a will to win, not a wish to win.
2. Inspiration.
3. Don't think you really win until you live up to that high thing within you, that makes you do your best, no matter what.
4. Never give up.
5. Desire, dedication and determination.
6. Fighting heart.
7. Strive for perfection.
8. Faith, confidence, courage, spirit and enthusiasm.

9. Self-control and patience.
10. Use your mind, concentration, visualisation.
11. Take defeat and bounce back to victory.
12. Take God with you.

These traits that separate the great players from the merely very good are not just exceptional but timeless. They have nothing to do with the quality of courses or the technical excellence of the game itself. Because of this, the greatest players must be drawn from across the history of championship golf. There are many to choose from yet there is only room for 100 golfers in this book. The list of those left out could be as long again. America has most representatives in the book, and probably most cause for complaint about those who have been omitted. Among those who might have been in were: Johnny McDermott, Macdonald Smith, Leo Diegel, Chick Evans, Craig Wood, Horton Smith, Denny Shute, Henry Picard, Paul Runyan, Ralph Guldahl, Lloyd Mangrum, Jackie Burke, Gene Littler, Doug Ford, Dave Stockton, Larry Nelson, Tom Weiskopf, Tom Kite, Lanny Wadkins, Lee Janzen, Mark O'Meara, Hal Sutton, Fred Couples, Davis Love, Steve Stricker and Jim Furyk. And of the women: Sandra Haynie, Judy Rankin, Pat Bradley, Patty Sheehan, Betsy King, Amy Alcott, Beth Daniel, Meg Mallon, plus Australia's Jan Stephenson, Sweden's Liselotte Neumann and Ayako Okamoto, from Japan.

From Britain: Jamie Anderson, Bob Ferguson, both three-time Open champions from the early days; Bob Martin, Willie Park Jnr, Andrew Kirkaldy, Willie Dunn, Sandy Herd, Abe Mitchell, Peter Alliss, Max Faulkner, Dai Rees, Neil Coles, Peter Oosterhuis and Paul Lawrie. And two home winners of the Women's British Open, Karen Stupples and Catriona Matthew, also merited consideration. From elsewhere: David Graham, Graham Marsh, Bruce Crampton, Chi-Chi Rodriguez, Eduardo Romero, Angel Cabrera, Miguel Angel Jimenez, Thomas Bjorn, Trevor Immelman, Geoff Ogilvy. Asia undoubtedly will have far more representatives in any future edition but Jumbo Ozaki, winner or over 100 titles in Japan but only the New Zealand PGA outside it, did not make it, nor did, although much closer, Korea's YE Yang, who beat Woods at the 2009 USPGA, and KJ Choi, the 2011 Players champion. Perhaps

Ryo Ishikawa, the Bashful Prince from Japan, will feature some day. Talking of really young stars, Italy's Matteo Manassero, the youngest player to win the Amateur Championship (16 years old) and to win a tournament on the European Tour (17 years old), is surely a certainty for future greatness.

Perhaps the biggest problem in assessing players for this book was in comparing players still active in their careers with those players of long ago. Generally, it was hard to include most of the current younger crop whose careers are still evolving, even such fine Englishmen as Paul Casey, Ian Poulter, Justin Rose and Luke Donald, although the last, after becoming the number one player in the world in 2011, was a contender. So were a number of recent major champions (all, of course, may well have more to come): Martin Kaymer, Louis Oosthuizen, Charl Schwartzel and Graeme McDowell. As the first European to win the US Open for 40 years, followed up by a starring role in the Ryder Cup of 2010, it was hard to leave McDowell out. It may be that Northern Ireland is under-represented given that Fred Daly, the 1947 Open champion, might also have made it.

But Darren Clarke and Rory McIlroy played their way into the book. By winning the Open at Royal St. George's with a magnificent display of links golf in testing conditions, Clarke capped a fine career that includes Ryder Cup glory and success at the World Golf Championship level. McIlroy is 20 years younger, and at just 22 years old his inclusion may be considered premature. Certainly, nothing created more debate when canvassing the views of others on McIlroy. There were those for and those against, but both sides stated their cases emphatically.

Clearly, a fuller appreciation of McIlroy's career will have to wait, but producing one of the greatest, most dominant major victories ever at the US Open, straight after blowing the Masters so miserably, qualifies McIlroy in my book. Look at the records McIlroy set at Congressional: the lowest total for a US Open by four strokes (previous holders included Nicklaus and Woods), the lowest totals for 36 and 54 holes, the first player to get to 13, 14, 15, 16 and 17 under par, and equal largest halfway lead. He was also the youngest US Open champion since Jones in 1923 and the youngest European winner of a major since Young Tom Morris in 1868. That's pretty good company to be keeping.

When something has not been done for almost a century or more, then that something must be pretty special. This was the achievement of another 22-year-old in 2011. Yani Tseng first became the youngest player to win four majors since Young Tom, then she became the youngest ever, male or female, to win five. She made the book, too.

Records such as these are not mere statistical niceties but provide a context in the form of what has gone before, and so gave an important suggestion as to how to lay out the order of the entries in this book. An alphabetical listing, or one using some arbitrary ranking system, would place players out of the context of their times. Great players are defined partly by who has gone before but mostly by the great players they played against. Take the battles of the Great Triumvirate, or the fact that once Jones started winning majors, Hagen and Sarazen only got a look in when Jones was not playing. Nelson and Hogan were the same age but Nelson's career was virtually over by the time Hogan got going. It was into the era of Arnie that Nicklaus began his incredible run, leaving others to judge themselves against the Golden Bear for the next couple of decades, just the way Els, Singh, Mickelson and Garcia are defined by having played in the era of Tiger Woods. In this way, the stories of golf's greatest players, from Allan Robertson to Rory McIlroy, reveal the excitement and drama underlying the momentous story of championship golf.

FROM THE PIONEERS
TO THE GREAT TRIUMVIRATE
1860–1900

With the establishment of the Open, now one of the modern game's four majors but initially from more humble beginnings in the second half of the 19th century, so came golf's first great heroes. A motley collection of mainly Scottish caddies, the game's first professionals, gathered each year to play for the Challenge Belt – although after Young Tom Morris had won this three times in a row, he was awarded it outright. The original trophy was replaced, after a year's hiatus, by the claret jug that is still competed for today – Young Tom won that as well, before dying at the tragically young age of 24.

These early days of the Open were a fascinating time, with John Ball becoming the first amateur winner. With Harold Hilton, another Open champion, and Freddie Tait also making their mark, the Amateur Championship quickly established itself as a coveted title. Golf reached its seminal moment, however, in the golden age of the Great Triumvirate. JH Taylor was the first to win the Open, while James Braid dominated over a short span. But Harry Vardon superseded both, winning the Claret Jug six times – still a record – as well as the US Open. With a swing that produced wonderfully consistent golf, he pioneered a new way of playing the game. There was no greater pioneer, however, than where the story starts, with Allan Robertson.

Allan Robertson

ALLAN ROBERTSON

Born September 11, 1815, St. Andrews, Fife;
died September 1, 1859, St. Andrews, Fife

As we have seen, while Allan Robertson lived the concept of championship golf did not exist. Instead, it was in money matches that Robertson earned his formidable reputation as the best player of the age. The St. Andrews man once beat Musselburgh's big-hitting Willie Dunn in a match of 20 rounds over ten days. It was said he never lost a singles match on even terms, while Robertson and his apprentice Tom Morris were unbeaten at foursomes. Robertson picked his duels, however, and never took up a standing challenge from Willie Park, nor went head-to-head with Morris once the latter reached his prime.

Acknowledged as the game's first professional, Robertson, like his father and grandfather before him, was a caddie for the members of the Royal and Ancient (R&A) and a maker of feathery golf balls (balls consisting of feathers in a leather casing), over 2,000 a year emerging from his kitchen and selling for half a crown each. He was also responsible for some of the key improvements to the Old Course and, in summer, he would rise at dawn to play the links, perhaps the first to develop his game by actually practising.

He was not a long hitter, but kept control of the ball and was deadly at running the ball up towards the hole. He was barred from entering the occasional competition for caddies – to give the others a chance. James Balfour, a prominent R&A member, described a 'short, little, active man, with a pleasant face and a merry twinkle in his eye. His style was neat and effective. With him the game was one of head as much as of hand; he always kept cool, and generally pulled through a match, even when he fell behind. He was a natural gentleman.'

But he was also a master of the dark arts, the game's first serious hustler. With the honour on the tee, he might make a great show of putting all his energy into a swing, only to hold back at the last minute and have his ball finish just short of a bunker. His opponent, believing trouble was out of reach, would inevitably knock his drive into the trap, and be praised for his great strength. On the final hole of a tight match, Robertson would remove his jacket, roll up his sleeves and spit on his hands – all designed to unsettle his rival. Or when partnering a weak club member who faced a dicey shot over severe trouble, he would persuade him to choose an air-shot, allowing Robertson to hit to safety rather than risk losing ball and hole.

'It's nae gowff,' Robertson said of the new gutty ball, a solid ball made from the Malaysian percha tree, that would make his feathery-making operation obsolete. Eventually accepting the change, he developed new techniques using iron-headed clubs, as opposed to the wooden-headed clubs then in use. In 1858 he birdied the final hole of the Old Course for a 79, the first time anyone had broken 80 on the links – hardly anyone else could break 100. A year later he was dead of jaundice, at the age of 44. 'They may toll the bells and shut up the shops at St. Andrews, for their greatest is gone,' said one tribute. It would be the following year before the annual crowning of the game's champion golfer would begin.

WILLIE PARK SNR

Born June 30, 1833, Musselburgh, East Lothian; died July 25, 1903, Scotland
Open champion 1860, '63, '66 and '75

The first staging of what is now called the Open Championship was at Prestwick in 1860. Eight caddies, who the following day would be back carrying the clubs of their amateur masters, contested the title over three rounds of the 12-hole course in one day. Tom Morris, the home professional, was the favourite. Willie Park, from Musselburgh, was the winner. He won by two strokes and was the first to claim the Challenge Belt, made of red Moroccan leather by Edinburgh silversmiths James & Walter Marshall. A replica was presented to South Africa's Louis Oosthuizen on winning the 150th anniversary Open at St. Andrews in 2010.

Park, the son of a farmer, learnt the game by playing with a whittled stick. He was a prodigiously long driver of the ball and

Willie Park Snr

a fine putter – he used the same club for both facets of the game. He arrived in St. Andrews in 1854 as a wiry youngster of 20 and challenged the great Allan Robertson to a game. Robertson never did play Park but a match was arranged with George Morris, Tom's brother. George was thrashed, losing the first eight holes, so Tom, now based in Prestwick, ventured east to regain family honour. He could not. Over rounds at St. Andrews, North Berwick and Musselburgh, Park prevailed.

The pair would battle many times over the decades, often part-nered by Tom's son, Tommy, and Willie's brother Mungo. In their last head-to-head match at Musselburgh in 1882, Park was two-up with six to play when the referee stopped the match because specta-tors were interfering with play. Morris and the referee retired to the pub but Park stayed out and sent word that, if they did not return, he would play the remaining holes anyway and claim the match. Which he did.

In the first nine Opens – amateurs were allowed to play from 1861 – Park won three times, finished runner-up four times and was never worse than fourth. He won a fourth title in 1875. Mungo Park, five years younger, also became Open champion in 1874, while Willie's son, Willie junior, was the champion in 1887 and '89. Willie junior then devoted more time to his club-making business and he became one of the first commercial course design-ers, with the Old Course at Sunningdale among his gems. He also wrote well on the game and said: 'The man who can putt is a match for anyone.' As a fine putter it applied to himself, as well as to his father.

As well as issuing a standing challenging to anyone in the world to a £100-a-side match, Willie Park Snr also took on club golfers while standing on one leg and playing one-handed. They say he only lost once. While putting, he was one of the first to stress the impor-tance of never leaving the ball short of the hole, in stark contrast to his great rival, Tom Morris.

OLD TOM MORRIS

Born June 16, 1821, St. Andrews, Fife;
died May 24, 1908, St. Andrews, Fife
Open champion 1861, '62, '64 and '67

Tom Morris's one flaw as a golfer was his putting. 'He would be a much better player,' his son chided, 'if the hole was a yard closer.' Worse, from close range he was shaky. A letter was once delivered to him successfully, addressed to 'The Misser of Short Putts, Prestwick'. He was not offended. As someone who lived to the age of 86 and survived his wife, daughter and three sons, perhaps he knew there were worse things in life than missing a few putts.

By the time of his death, from a fall down the stairs at the New Club in St. Andrews, Morris was much loved as the game's 'Grand Old Man'. His influence on the game outweighed anyone else's in the second half of the 19th century. He first started playing golf in St. Andrews as a six-year-old. He was an apprentice of Allan Robertson but they fell out for a time when he was found using the new gutty ball, which his employer had banned.

Morris went to Prestwick in 1851 as Keeper of the Green, establishing the course that would host the first 12 Opens. He was runner-up in the first of them but then won a year later and the year after that by 13 strokes, a record for major championships that would stand until Tiger Woods won the 2000 US Open by 15 strokes. He won again in 1864, the year he returned to St. Andrews to become Keeper of the Green on the Old Course, paid a salary of £50 a year by the R&A. The course we know today essentially evolved under Old Tom's care.

He also laid out many other courses, including the New Course at St. Andrews, Carnoustie, Muirfield, Dornoch and County Down. He influenced some of the finest course architects, including Donald Ross, Charles Blair Macdonald and Harry Colt, while Dr Alister Mackenzie studied his work extensively.

Morris was a man of deep religious conviction and established the convention that the Old Course should be rested on a Sunday. He also bathed in the sea, summer and winter, east coast or west,

Old Tom Morris

every day. Horace Hutchinson described his golfing style: 'There is a great deal of body swing in his driving stroke. It is a rather slow swing, the kind of swing that permits a man to use a rather supple club. Tom's clubs are supple and flat in the lie and his swing is a flat one, rather of the "auld wife cutting hay" style, according to Bob Martin's description of his own fine driving manner – generally sending the ball away with a fine flat trajectory that gives a good run.'

After the death of Robertson, Morris and Willie Park were the pre-eminent professionals of the time – until his son, Tommy, came along. Tommy was dashing and daring, everything his father was not. 'I could cope with Allan myself,' Old Tom said, 'but never with Tommy.' In 1867, at the age of 46 years and 99 days, Old Tom won his fourth Open title and remains the oldest ever winner.

YOUNG TOM MORRIS
Born April 20, 1851, St. Andrews, Fife;
died December 25, 1875, St. Andrews, Fife
Open champion 1868, '69, '70 and '72

In 1868, at the age of 17 years, five months and eight days, Tommy Morris – later to be written into golfing legend as 'Young Tom' – won his first Open and remains the youngest ever winner. He was aided by the championship's first hole-in-one on Prestwick's eighth hole. Once he started winning, he did not stop. He won the next year and again in 1870, when his three-round, 36-hole score was 149, which remained the lowest ever until the championship expanded to 72 holes in 1892. He won by 12 strokes and *The Field* reported: 'His play was excellent. In fact, we never saw golf clubs handled so beautifully.'

Under the rules bequeathing the Challenge Belt, anyone winning it three times in a row was allowed to keep it. The belt remained on the Morris sideboard until Old Tom's death in 1908, when it was relocated to the R&A clubhouse. There was no Open in 1871. With

Young Tom Morris

no trophy to play for, once again, as in the days of Allan Robertson, golf had an undisputed champion.

When the Open resumed in 1872, with a new silver claret jug to play for, Morris won again, and remains the only player to win four times in succession. He was the game's original boy wonder. He first started hitting balls on the beach at Prestwick but his game really developed after the family returned to St. Andrews. Aged 13, he accompanied his father to a tournament in Perth but played in a private match against a local boy. His score would have won the official competition. Aged 16, he beat all the professionals at Carnoustie, winning a playoff against Willie Park and Bob Andrew.

Young Tom never cared for the deferential life of a club caddie. Instead, he saw himself solely as a player. 'His exuberant address and slashing full swing was regarded as the only model for a first class player,' wrote contemporary golf author Garden Smith, who added that notions of 'slow back', 'keep your eye on the ball' and 'stand firm on your legs' were 'conspicuous by their absence'.

In 1874, Tommy married Margaret Drinnen and in September the following year they were expecting their first child. Tommy and his father went off to play against the Park brothers at North Berwick but word came that they should return home. They sailed back that night but it was too late. Meg and the baby had died in childbirth. Tommy was distraught with grief. He played golf only twice more, the last time in a six-day, 12-round match in December. They played through snowstorms and Tommy won but, now drinking heavily, his health was deteriorating. He was found on the morning of Christmas Day, dead of a ruptured artery that had bled into his lungs – although the romantic legend endures that he died of a broken heart.

He was buried in the cemetery in the grounds of the ruined St. Andrews cathedral, walking distance from the Old Course. A monument was erected with the inscription: 'Deeply regretted by numerous friends and all golfers. He thrice in succession won the champion's Belt and held it without rivalry and yet without envy. His many amiable qualities being no less acknowledged than his golfing achievements.'

JOHN BALL

Born December 24, 1861, Hoylake, Cheshire;
died December 2, 1940, Holywell, Flintshire
Open champion 1890; Amateur champion 1888,
'90, '92, '94, '99, 1907, '10 and '12

If Young Tom was the first player we would recognise today as a tournament professional, John Ball was the opposite – the game's first great amateur champion. His father was the owner of the Royal Hotel at Hoylake, which provided the headquarters for the Royal Liverpool Golf Club when it was founded in 1869. Ball was eight at the time and living on the edge of the links immediately gave him a new passion. He was talented and proficient enough to finish tied for fourth place in the Open at Prestwick in 1878 as a 16-year-old (some texts say he was 14 but the dates suggest otherwise).

As a prize he received ten shillings, a payment which became relevant when his club decided to put on a national championship for amateur players in 1885. The only problem was that no one knew quite what an amateur was. The suggestion was someone who did not take prize money from a competition, which ruled out the Elie stonemason Douglas Rolland, who was runner-up at the 1884 Open and accepted the prize. But what about Ball, the host club's ace? The club decided to place a statute of limitation on the acceptance of prize money and Ball was cleared to enter.

While the Open was played under the medal, or strokeplay, format, the Amateur was a knockout under the matchplay format, holes won and lost. It was a test of nerve and Ball was uniquely suited to it. He reached the semi-finals that year and went on to win a never-to-be-matched eight Amateur titles between 1888 and 1912, when he was past his 50th year. As a 60-year-old he reached the last 16, a remarkably lengthy career given it covered the Boer War, during which he served with Cheshire Yeomanry and did not play golf for three years, as well as the First World War.

Ball's greatest year was 1890 when he won his second Amateur title and then became the first amateur, and the first Englishman, to win the Open. It was at Prestwick, where the course had been extended to 18

12

holes. Having not played in the event for 12 years, he posted two scores of 82 and beat Willie Fernie and Archie Simpson by three strokes. His triumph did much to popularise the championship in England, where hitherto it had been considered an event for Scottish professionals.

Only Bobby Jones has ever equalled Ball's feat of winning the Open and the Amateur in the same year, and the only other amateur to win the Open was Harold Hilton, a fellow Hoylake member. While Ball, who retired to a North Wales farm, was undemonstrative, except for his exceptional golf, and shy, Hilton was a man of words. Hilton the historian wrote that Ball 'was the very first player to impress upon the world the possibilities of iron play. He was the only amateur in those early days who regularly played the ball straight at the pin, shot after shot. The majority were content to place the ball somewhere on the putting green, but he always seemed to play direct for the hole. At the time he was looked upon as a phenomenon whose play could only be admired, not imitated.'

When Ball won his sixth Amateur at St. Andrews in 1907 he was made an honorary member of the R&A. He never won a second Open, but contended again in 1892, when he was the third-round leader but lost to a member of his own club, one Harold Hilton.

HAROLD HILTON

Born January 14, 1869, West Kirby, Cheshire;
died March 5, 1942 (location unconfirmed)
Open champion 1892 and '97; Amateur champion 1900,
'01, '11 and '13; US Amateur champion 1911

Harold Hilton was born in the same year that his club, Royal Liverpool, was founded. His decision to play in the 1892 Open was a late one. He took the overnight train to Edinburgh, arriving on the day before but in time to play three practice rounds over the new links of Muirfield. There was also a new format, with four rounds over two days. The change brought the best out of England's great amateurs but may have been rued by Horace Hutchinson,

13

John Ball

HAROLD
HILTON

twice winner of the Amateur and, like Hilton, one of the game's great historians, who led after the first day.

Hilton was seven behind at that stage but a brilliant 72 in the third round put him two behind John Ball. Hilton's 74 to Ball's 79 in the final round denied Ball a second Open title and when the Open was staged at their home club of Hoylake for the first time in 1897, Hilton triumphed again. This time Hilton overtook James Braid in the final round but had been an earlier starter, so he played billiards while waiting for Braid to finish one stroke adrift.

No British amateur has won the Open since. Hilton was a small but powerful man. Golf writer Bernard Darwin described his style as a 'little man jumping on his toes and throwing himself and his club after the ball with almost frenetic abandon.' Others said he looked like a 'schoolboy giving the ball a really good smack'. Often his cap was dislodged in the process, but doubtless the ever-present cigarette remained in place.

However, the example of Ball, his elder club-mate, and playing on the Hoylake links ensured Hilton learnt to play with control. Not long off the tee, Hilton was a superb striker of long approach shots with wooden clubs. He also showed exceptional touch around the greens.

It was said he was better at medal play than matchplay but he won the Amateur four times, starting with back-to-back titles in 1900 and '01, and was a runner-up three times. In 1911, at the age of 42, he enjoyed one of the great seasons in golf when he won a third Amateur title, finished third at the Open and then became the first overseas winner of the US Amateur at Apawamis in New York. He was the first to win both Amateur titles in the same year and the last British winner of the US version until Richie Ramsay replicated the feat in 2006.

In 1911 Hilton became founding editor of *Golf Monthly* magazine, while he also went on to be editor of *Golf Illustrated*. One of his perks in 1914 was deciding the pairings for the *Golf Illustrated* Gold Vase, a warm-up for the Amateur. Hilton put himself alongside the visiting American Francis Ouimet, the sensational winner of the US Open the previous year. The hospitality went no further and Hilton was the winner. Along with Ball, Hilton ranks as one of Britain's greatest amateurs but if he had a nemesis, it was the son of an Edinburgh professor.

FREDDIE TAIT

Born January 11, 1870, Edinburgh;
died February 7, 1900, Koodoosberg, South Africa
Amateur champion 1896 and '98

There was no loss of honour, for Harold Hilton or anybody else, in losing to Freddie Tait. Both times Tait won the Amateur Championship he beat Hilton, in the final in 1896 and in the fourth round two years later when Hilton was the reigning Open champion. A lieutenant in the Black Watch, Tait was not just a crack rifle shot but also a fine rugby player and cricketer, as well as a golfer from an early age. He was the third son of Professor Peter Tait, of Edinburgh University, who was a member of the R&A and spent his summers in St. Andrews playing up to five rounds a day.

Once, the professor experimented with playing at night after coating some balls in phosphorescent paint. Alas, the round came to an end when the hand of a playing partner was burned after the flammable paint set his glove alight. He also had a theory that a gutty ball could not be hit further than 191 yards, but on a frosty morning in 1893 his son reached the green at the 13th hole of the Old Course with a blow of 341 yards. The same year Freddie scored a 72 on the Old, although it did not count as a new record since it was not from the medal tees.

Tait was known for his long driving and was sometimes crooked but made the most remarkable recoveries. He sounds like the Seve Ballesteros of his day, described by Bernard Darwin as a 'very great golfer with a certain exciting quality in his game that has never been surpassed.' When one drive veered off line and through a spectator's hat, the irritated wearer requested compensation. After Tait complained at forking out five shillings, Old Tom Morris told him: 'You ought to be glad it was only a new hat you had to buy and not an oak coffin.'

Tait was steady enough at medal play to finish in the top nine at the Open in five out of six years, twice being third and four times ranking as the best amateur. But he was at his best in the head-to-head format. If he had Hilton's number, Tait himself had some titanic matches against Hoylake's other great champion, John Ball.

Freddie Tait

They met in the final of the 1899 Amateur at Prestwick and Ball only triumphed at the 37th hole. It was Tait's last appearance in the championship, although a few weeks later he got revenge on Ball in a match at Royal Lytham after being four-down with 13 holes to play. It was his last match. That autumn, he sailed to South Africa for the Boer War and was shot dead leading a charge at Koodoosberg. The R&A's history, *Champions & Guardians*, says the news was 'received with stunned disbelief, not just by the golfing world, for Tait was a household name and he was everybody's hero. His infectious humour, his high spirits and his friendly disposition were combined with generosity and modesty, all of which endeared him to fellow soldiers and fellow golfers alike.'

In the affections of the golfing world Tait, who passed away aged just 30, was a third great amateur along with Ball and Hilton. Soon, however, three great professionals would overshadow all.

JH TAYLOR

Born March 19, 1871, Northam, Devon;
died February 10, 1963, Northam, Devon
Open champion 1894, '95, 1900, '09 and '13

Over the two decades up to the First World War the game was dominated by the Great Triumvirate of JH Taylor, Harry Vardon and James Braid. The trio won 16 out of 21 Open Championships and in the five other years one, or even two, of them were second. John Henry Taylor, known as 'JH', became the first English professional to win, in 1894 at Sandwich, the first time the Open was staged outside Scotland, and he retained the title at St. Andrews. A hat-trick of victories was only prevented by Vardon after a 36-hole playoff at Muirfield in 1896.

Taylor grew up near the great links of Royal North Devon at Westward Ho! and learned the game as a caddie and greenkeeper. Having left school at the age of 11, he worked as a boot boy, a gardener's boy and a builder's labourer. Of the Triumvirate, Taylor

JH Taylor

was the first to blossom, finishing tenth when he, and Vardon, made their Open debuts in 1893.

By nature and nurture, Taylor was ideally suited to the challenge of battling the elements on the links. He was stockily built and had a low, flat, punchy swing which kept the ball under the wind, something he had many hours to perfect at Westward Ho! It was said of him: 'When he pulled down his cap, stuck out his chin and embedded his large boots in the ground, he could hit straight through the wind as though it were not there.'

Taylor was in the top ten at the Open for 17 straight years, was a runner-up six times and the champion five times, equalling Braid and one short of Vardon's record. His greatest performance came at St. Andrews in 1900 when, uniquely, he returned the lowest score in each round to beat Vardon by eight strokes with Braid five further adrift in third place. The same year he was runner-up to Vardon at the US Open while two more Open titles arrived in 1909 and '13, the latter at the age of 42.

For over 40 years Taylor was the professional at Royal Mid-Surrey and, as well as helping to found the Artisan Golfers' Association and the Public Golf Courses Association, he was the father of the Professional Golfers' Association. Bernard Darwin credited him with 'turning a feckless company into a self-respecting and respected body of men.' A natural leader, Taylor was the non-playing captain when Britain won the Ryder Cup at Southport and Ainsdale in 1933. Although his formal schooling was brief, he was a superb speaker and became a gifted writer, forsaking a 'ghost' for his acclaimed autobiography, *Golf, My Life's Work*.

Along with Braid and 1893 Open champion Willie Auchterlonie, he was among the first professionals elected as honorary members of the R&A in 1950. Having retired to a home on the hill overlooking Westward Ho!, where the view he said was the 'finest in all of Christendom', Taylor received what he regarded as his greatest honour when he was made president of Royal North Devon in 1957. For a brief period, Taylor had been the best player in the game, but that ended the day in 1896, as a double reigning Open champion, when he was defeated 8 and 6 (over 36 holes) at Ganton by the club's young professional.

HARRY VARDON

Born May 9, 1870, Grouville, Jersey;
died March 20, 1937, Totteridge, Hertfordshire
Open champion 1896, '98, '99, 1903, '11 and '14;
US Open champion 1900

He might have given JH Taylor a couple of years start, but once Harry Vardon began winning, he found it difficult to stop. While there was then no organised tour outside the majors, one estimate suggests at one point Vardon won 17 tournaments out of 22, and finished runner-up in the other five. His place in the game's history is secured by his six Open victories, a record yet to be matched. In three appearances in the US Open, Vardon finished first, second, second. As a great champion who popularised the game, Vardon was the natural successor to Young Tom Morris, but his impact was all the greater for his triumphs on both sides of the Atlantic. 'I do not think anyone who saw him in his prime, will disagree as to this, that a greater golfing genius is inconceivable,' wrote Bernard Darwin.

Vardon started as a caddie at Grouville, near St. Helier on Jersey. His father always thought his brother Tom was the better golfer but Harry became the better winner. Tom, who was the professional at Royal St. George's before moving to America, never won the Open but was second in 1903, inevitably to Harry. That was the year Harry suffered from fainting fits and was later diagnosed with tuberculosis. He often suffered from ill health, but it was the saving of him in 1912 when he had to cancel a trip to America, having been booked to sail on the Titanic.

His slim frame belied the length he possessed off the tee. His was an easy style, both elegant and effective. His upright swing was in contrast to the popular 'St. Andrews swing', where the club was swept around the body. Vardon's success changed the mechanics of the swing forever. He also used the overlapping grip where the little finger of the right hand covers the index finger of the left. He was not the first player to use it, but the most famous; hence it became known as the 'Vardon grip'.

The key to Vardon's game was his accuracy. Taylor said: 'Vardon played fewer shots out of the rough than anyone who has ever swung a golf club. If the test of a player be that he makes fewer bad shots than the remainder, then I give Vardon the palm. He hit the ball in the centre of every club with greater frequency than any other player, and in this most difficult feat lay his great strength as a player.' His relative weakness was his putting. He was fine on the approach putts but suffered over the short ones – the 'jumps' he called it; we would say the 'yips' today. 'I think I know as well as anyone how not to do it,' he said.

In 1900, when he beat Taylor to win the US Open at Chicago, Vardon embarked on a nine-month tour of America, playing exhibitions and making appearances at sporting goods stores on behalf of equipment manufacturer Spalding. Everywhere he drew crowds and there was a significant advance in interest in the game, just as there was when he returned in 1913, but he lost, along with Ted Ray, in a playoff to the 20-year-old amateur Francis Ouimet, perhaps the game's greatest giant-killing act. Vardon was 50 when he returned to the USA in 1920 and almost won the title back.

Taylor said Vardon, the long-time professional at South Herts, was always the 'most courteous and delightful of opponents', giving the 'fullest possible credit' to the winner when defeated. 'To know him was to love him,' Taylor added.

JAMES BRAID

Born February 6, 1870, Earlsferry, Fife;
died November 27, 1950, London
Open champion 1901, '05, '06, '08 and '10

James Braid had to wait longer than his contemporaries for his own glory days but, once they arrived, his achievements fully justified expanding the designation of 'greatest' to a 'triumvirate'. For 14 years in a row he was in the top five at the Open. He won his first title in 1901 and then from 1905 won four times in six years to become

JAMES BRAID

the first player to claim the title five times, quite a feat given the head start he had given JH Taylor and Harry Vardon, and that they were his chief opponents. Only Taylor, Peter Thomson and Tom Watson have matched the feat, and only Vardon has surpassed it. Braid also won the fledgling British Professional Matchplay Championship, sponsored by the *News of the World*, four times in nine years.

Braid grew up at Elie, near St. Andrews, the son of a ploughman, and he hardly had the advantages of others in such fertile golfing territory. It was only when he moved down to London to work as an apprentice clubmaker for the Army & Navy Stores that his golfing education took off – for one thing, he could play on his day off on Sundays, which religion prevented him from doing at home.

He developed a powerful swing and drove the ball huge distances but without Vardon's accuracy. Braid was a stoic, calm sort of chap but his golf was exciting to watch and he had a popular following, always anticipating whatever might happen next, not least his trademark recoveries. Horace Hutchinson said he played with a 'divine fury'. When he won at Muirfield in 1901, his opening tee shot sailed over a stone wall and out of bounds. By the time he got to the 72nd hole, he had plenty of shots in hand, which could have been a blessing when, playing his approach of 200 years, the shaft of his club splintered, sending his clubhead towards the clubhouse – fortunately the ball finished up safely on the green.

His greatest performance came at Prestwick in 1908 when he compiled scores of 70, 72, 77 and 72 for a total of 291, five better than the Open had seen before. He won by eight and his record score stood until 1927. Throughout his decade of success, Park's putting was sublime, while his touch around the green was always delicate for such a tall man with large hands.

Once Walton Heath opened in 1904, Braid became the club professional for 45 years. He also went on to become the most sought-after golf course architect of the 1920s and '30s. Among his classics are the King's and Queen's courses at Gleneagles. More reserved than Vardon or Taylor, Braid nonetheless played an equal part in the Great Triumvirate's achievements, both on the course and in raising interest in the game generally. 'He was an immensely painstaking man of few words, a warm and true friend,' was one tribute.

Arnaud Massy

Born July 6, 1877 Biarritz, France;
died April 16, 1950, Etretat, France
Open champion 1907

The five men, other than the Great Triumvirate, who claimed the Open between 1894 and 1914 were the English amateur Harold Hilton (his second victory), two Scots in Sandy Herd and Jack White, the Channel Islander Ted Ray – and a Frenchman. Arnaud Massy was, in the words of Hilton, 'the first stranger within our gates to annex the blue ribbon of our golfing world, and none can say that he was not fully worthy of the honour.'

Golf was not unknown in France – the club at Pau, near the Pyrenees, has recently celebrated its 150th anniversary – but it was mainly provided for the pleasure of visiting Britons. The only set of clubs right-handed Massy could find when he was learning the game were left-handed. More usually, left-handers were forced to play right-handed due to the unavailability of left-handed sets, although Phil Mickelson is a natural righty who learnt as a lefty by standing opposite his father and mirroring his swing.

In 1902 Massy moved to North Berwick, switched round to playing right-handed and really started practising, although there was time to marry a local lass. His great year was 1907. Early in the year, he beat a number of British players in tournaments staged on the Riviera and won his second successive French Open, while at the end of the season he defeated James Braid over 36-holes at Deal. In between, the Frenchman denied Braid a third successive Open victory at Hoylake.

In fact, though, it was JH Taylor who was Massy's chief opponent in the 1907 Open. Taylor led by one with a round to play but Massy's 77 to Taylor's 80 brought victory by two strokes to France, for the first and so far last time. Continental Europe had to wait until 1979 for Seve Ballesteros and its next Open champion. A strong wind and occasional lashing rain made that year's championship the 'very finest test of the game,' according to Hilton, yet Massy 'rose superior to the trying conditions and seemed less affected by them than any of his rivals. One of the great virtues of his style is the firmness of

Arnaud
Massy

his stance and apparent control of balance. I cannot call to mind any player who seems quite as firm on his feet as Arnaud Massy.'

Massy was also a fine putter, and according to the *Shell Encyclopaedia of Golf*, 'he held himself like a Grenadier and made the most of his mighty chest, playing with a fine, ferocious gaiety that made him a most attractive golfer.' The gaiety was misplaced when he faced Harry Vardon in a 36-hole playoff for the Open at Sandwich in 1911. Well behind playing the then par-three 17th in the afternoon, Massy hit his tee shot to 12 feet only to see Vardon get inside him. Although under strokeplay rules the round should have been completed, Massy conceded. Perhaps apocryphally, he is said to have muttered on the way back to the clubhouse, 'I cannot play zis damn game.'

Later, returning to France, he became the professional at Chantaco. He won four French Opens in all (and was the runner-up three times), plus the Spanish Open three times and the Belgian Open once. In an era where three men dominated, one Frenchman emphatically made his mark.

TED RAY

Born March 28, 1877, Grouville, Jersey;
died August 26, 1943, London
Open champion 1912; US Open champion 1920

Ted Ray was a hard man to overshadow, even for the Great Triumvirate. He was, after all, a 'huge, lumbering figure of a man with a pipe invariably clenched between his teeth, a trilby hat on his head and a philosophy reflected in the advice he once gave a golfer who wanted to hit the ball further: "Hit it a bloody sight harder, mate."' Ray is also one of only three Britons to have won the Open and the US Open.

He grew up in the same village on Jersey as Harry Vardon, seven years the master's junior. His start was as a caddie at Royal Jersey but it was not long before he followed Vardon to the mainland,

TED RAY

eventually succeeding him as the professional at Ganton in 1903. Like everyone else at the time, he had to be patient in waiting for success to arrive but Ray had a determination to improve, and in 1912 at Muirfield he finally won the claret jug, impressively by four strokes from Vardon and by eight from Braid.

Ray was the perfect foil for Vardon when they toured America together in 1913, ultimately losing in a playoff for the US Open to the unheralded Francis Ouimet. Among those who marvelled at the pair, when they played an exhibition at East Lake in Atlanta, was a young Bobby Jones, who admired Vardon's accuracy and steadiness but was astonished by Ray's power.

Where Vardon swung effortlessly, Ray gave it the kitchen sink. His swing was like the 'lurching charge of an enraged Cape buffalo,' according to one observer. Ray was the biggest hitter of his age, but often erratic, so he developed a fine recovery game. The friends returned to America in 1920 when Vardon, at the age of 50, led the US Open before a late collapse. The highly-strung Leo Diegel also had a chance but imploded and Ray was the beneficiary. In 1970 Tony Jacklin joined Vardon and Ray as the only Britons to have won both Opens, while Graeme McDowell is the only other to win the US version in modern times.

Ray, who had moved to Oxhey in Hertfordshire in 1912, was made an honorary member of the club, a singular tribute for a professional at the time. He remained at the club until shortly before his death, and was always a popular figure. At the age of 50 he was the playing captain of the Ryder Cup team. A fast walker, as well as a fast swinger, he would not have enjoyed the modern trend for deliberate play (i.e. far too slow) by today's professionals. 'To think when we ought to play is madness,' he said.

No foreign player (at least who wasn't a nationalised American) won the US Open again until Gary Player in 1965. Yet quite apart from the victories of Vardon and Ray in America's national championship, its early days were dominated by players born in Britain, but who had made their home in the US.

American birth and the Age of the Emperor
1900–1930

American golf is indebted to the many hundreds of Scots who became the first professionals in the country and popularised the game. Many shared a first name with Willie Anderson, who is the only player to win the US Open three times in a row and shares the record of four titles in all. Yet the US Open was established as long ago as 1895, while American golf only really took off after Francis Ouimet, a 20-year-old amateur, won the competition in 1913. Not only was it his debut in the championship – and since then only Ben Curtis and Keegan Bradley have won a major on their first attempt – in the playoff he defeated the mighty British professionals Harry Vardon and Ted Ray. It was a sensation.

Soon Walter Hagen and Gene Sarazen emerged, but this was the Age of the Emperor, Bobby Jones. Learning the game from his Scottish professional at the Atlanta Athletic Club, Stewart Maiden, Jones became the most famous golfer in the world. In 1930 he claimed the Grand Slam – the Open and Amateur titles of both Britain and America. His feat has never been repeated and possibly never will. Having completed all he set out to do, he retired, but his legacy to the game includes Augusta National and the Masters tournament. Jones himself, however, said he was outclassed by the first great woman player, Joyce Wethered, who rose to prominence in an emerging women's game in the 1920s.

Willie Anderson

WILLIE ANDERSON

Born October 21, 1879, North Berwick, East Lothian;
died October 25, 1910, Philadelphia, Pennsylvania
US Open champion 1901, '03, '04 and '05

If you were Scottish, a golf professional and named 'Willie' there was a job for you in America at the end of the 19th century. Willie Anderson was one to make the transatlantic crossing and became the first man to win the US Open four times. The feat has never been beaten and only equalled by Bobby Jones, Ben Hogan and Jack Nicklaus.

Anderson was part of a mass emigration. Around 250 men from Carnoustie alone were said to have gone to America. Willie Smith, one of four brothers from the town, set up at Midlothian in Illinois, with brother Alex at Nassau in New York; Willie Campbell became the professional at The Country Club in Brookline, Willie Davis at Newport, Rhode Island and Willie Dunn at Shinnecock Hills.

Dunn's father was the Willie Dunn who had challenged Allan Robertson and Old Tom Morris. The son had originally gone to France, building courses in Biarritz, and was said to have taught more earls, lords and duchesses than any other professional. He also met WK Vanderbilt, who persuaded him over to New York. In 1894 Dunn won a so-called 'Open' matchplay competition, beating Campbell in the final, but in the first official Open run by the newly created United States Golf Association, he lost by two strokes to Horace Rawlins, who originated from the Isle of Wight.

Anderson was from North Berwick, where his father Tom was the greenkeeper, but was only 14 or so when he was persuaded to go to America by Frank Legh Slazenger, one of the sporting goods family who set up in New York. He taught the members at Misquamicut in Rhode Island, while practising his own game, and in 1897 was runner-up to Joe Lloyd in the US Open, starting a sequence of 11 top-five finishes in 14 years, his worst result being 15th.

His first win came at Myopia Hunt in 1901, beating Alex Smith in the first playoff at a US Open. Anderson was respected and admired by his peers but was generally a dour man, though on the first morning of the championship his ire was piqued by a club member who announced that the professionals, who were not allowed in the clubhouse at a US Open until Ted Ray's win in 1920, would be eating in the kitchen. Anderson was swishing a club and started to do so with more intensity until he slammed the club into the lawn and spat: 'Nae, nae. We're nae goin t' eat in the kitchen.' A tent was hastily erected.

Anderson won in another playoff in 1903 and then won again the following two years, the only hat-trick of victories the US Open has seen. He also won four Western Opens, at the time another big tournament. He was said to have played with great accuracy but his personality never shone through his golf. 'They don't know me,' Anderson would wail at his lack of any wider recognition. He died young, officially from arteriosclerosis, probably caused by heavy drinking, just days after completing a series of exhibitions in 1910.

WALTER TRAVIS

Born January 10, 1862, Maldon, Australia;
died July 31, 1927, Denver, Colorado
US Amateur champion 1900, '01 and '03;
British Amateur champion 1904

The first American champion on British soil was an Australian. Walter Travis went to America as a youngster and only turned to a sporting life late in the day. He was 34 or 35 when he decided to see how successful he could be at golf if he applied himself fully. Within two years of taking up the game he was a semi-finalist in the US Amateur and won the title at the age of 38 in 1900. A small man, always puffing on a black cigar, Travis was a short hitter but a deadly putter. He retained his title a year later despite the championship being interrupted for a week by the assassination of President McKinley.

Travis was an early adopter of the Haskell, the new rubber-wound ball with a solid core devised by Coburn Haskell, of Cleveland. These new balls ran much further than the old gutties but were dismissed as 'Bounding Billies' until Travis's success. A year later Sandy Herd won the Open using a Haskell – the same ball all four rounds, which was unheard of with a gutty – despite having denounced the innovation until he saw John Ball play with one in a practice round the day before the championship.

A third US Amateur title in four years followed in 1903 and the following year Travis journeyed to Sandwich for the British version. Unwittingly, he caused another stir with his equipment. His putting, the strength of his game, had gone off, and just before the event he borrowed from an American colleague a putter, the centre-shafted, mallet-headed Schenectady putter. Suddenly, he re-found his game and beat Harold Hilton and Horace Hutchinson before meeting the very long-hitting Edward Blackwell in the final. Blackwell had the advantage off the tee but was simply putted off the course.

A few years later the centre-shafted putter was banned by the R&A in Britain, although Travis still used it in America. However, he admitted: 'I have never been able to do anything with it since. I have tried repeatedly but it seems to have lost all its virtue.' It was eventually retired to a display cabinet at the Garden City club in New York where Travis was a member and redesigned the course. Many years later it was stolen during a party and was never returned. In 1908, Travis played Jerome Travers in the semi-finals of the US Amateur at his home club but came to grief at the 18th in a nasty pit bunker he had inserted by the green and which was particularly despised by his fellow members. Two swipes and the ball had not emerged, so he had to concede.

Travis never felt his historic victory at Sandwich was appreciated by the locals. But Hilton wrote: 'There may have been more brilliant players performing in that championship but there were none who exhibited more consistent accuracy than the American champion did. If ever a man deserved his success, it was Mr Travis at Sandwich. His game right through the event was the acme of applied science.'

JEROME TRAVERS

Born May 19, 1887, New York City, New York;
died March 29, 1951, East Hartford, Connecticut
US Amateur champion 1907, '08, '12, and '13;
US Open champion 1915

Despite their age gap, Jerry Travers had many great battles with Walter Travis, and the younger man was often the victor. Travers mirrored Travis in many departments of the game, being a shaky driver, often resorting to iron-headed clubs off the tee, but being a magical putter. He even copied Travis and successfully took up with the Schenectady putter.

Travers was born into a wealthy New York family and learned the game on their estate at Oyster Bay on Long Island – with the Carnoustie-born Alex Smith, the 1906 US Open champion (and again in 1910) brought in for expert tuition. His game was well suited to matchplay and he won the US Amateur in 1907 and '08, but the following year did not bother to enter. Seduced by the bright lights of Broadway, he was a handsome playboy who only played serious golf when the mood took.

Yet by winning four US Amateurs in all – only Bobby Jones has won more – and then the US Open in 1915, Travers was clearly one of the greatest golfers of his time. But his victory at Baltusrol was the last time he took part in a national championship. He retired to concentrate on being a cotton broker on Wall Street but he was later ruined in the stock market crash during the Great Depression. He turned professional but was unsuccessful, and spent the last ten years of his life as an airplane engine inspector for Pratt & Whitney. He did attend Jones's grand slam-sealing US Amateur victory in 1930 at Merion, paying as any other spectator. When he said no player came near to Jones, a companion suggested Travers himself might have done, but he replied: 'He could give me strokes and beat me on the best day I ever saw.'

Travers was not the only early American golfing hero to fade away quickly. Johnny McDermott won the US Open as a 19-year-old in 1911 and retained the title a year later. But within two years

Jerome Travers

McDermott had suffered a nervous breakdown and lived the rest of his life, dying one month short of his 80th birthday, cared for by his family and in rest homes.

When Chick Evans, who was the opposite of Travers, a great striker of the ball but a poor putter, won the US Open in 1916, three amateurs had won in four years. Only two more ever did, including Jones. Perhaps the first was the most remarkable, achieved by a young man who gave Travers his most fearsome challenge on the way to his fourth Amateur title in 1913. After the match, Travers sat down with the 20-year-old Francis Ouimet and talked though the match, providing a lifetime's golfing education in an hour. 'It may have been this wholehearted kindness to a novice competitor,' wrote Mark Frost in *The Greatest Game Ever Played*, 'that did more to alter the essential history of the game than the many great accomplishments Jerry Travers delivered on the course.'

FRANCIS OUIMET

Born May 8, 1893, Brookline, Massachusetts;
died September 2, 1967, Newton, Massachusetts
US Open champion 1913; US Amateur champion 1914 and '31

Francis Ouimet's victory in the 1913 US Open changed the history of the game in the United States. Golf was now an American sport, not merely an imported British pastime. Here an American hero was born, the 20-year-old unknown defeating the mighty Harry Vardon and Ted Ray. It was a fairytale win, the original Cinderella story (for *Caddyshack* fans) but also, said golf writer Bernard Darwin, 'the most momentous in all golf history'. Darwin was not only there at Brookline, he was the marker for the playoff. So taken was he with Ouimet that he could not help hoping the youngster would prevail.

Ouimet almost did not play. He had impressed at that year's US Amateur but was worried he would not get any more time off from his job as a clerk in a sporting goods store in Boston, although he

Francis Ouimet

did hope to get a glimpse of Vardon and Ray. Robert Watson, the president of the USGA, nonetheless put his name in the draw and his boss said: 'As well as you are entered, you had better plan to play.'

Ouimet lived across Clyde Street from The Country Club at Brookline. Looking out over the 17th fairway from his bedroom window and collecting lost balls sparked his interest in the game. He and his brother played on a crude course amid the rubble of the backyard. Later he played at a local public course or sneaked on to The Country Club at 4.30 in the morning, until a greenkeeper shooed him off. He caddied at the club and one day a member asked him to play. Caddies were expressly banned from playing but the caddiemaster turned a blind eye, as he did when other members started asking to play with the youngster.

He was the son of a French-Canadian father and an Irish mother, hardly the background of the other amateurs in the field. But rounds of 77, 74 and 74 put him level with Vardon and Ray. All three had 79s in the last round, played in the rain, with Ouimet birdying the 17th hole (and single-putting the last four holes) to force the tie. The following day he won the playoff with a score of 72 to Vardon's 77 and Ray's 78. Throughout, he was constantly encouraged by his ten-year-old caddie, Eddie Lowery, no bigger than the bag but who continually urged his man to: 'Be sure and keep your eye on the ball.'

If Ouimet's reception from the gallery had been rapturous the day before, now it bordered on the hysterical. The young champion was hoisted onto his supporters' shoulders and paraded in front of the clubhouse. At one point they stopped and Ouimet lowered his head as a woman whispered in his ear. Then he said: 'Thank you, mother. I'll be home soon.'

Robert Sommers, the USGA historian, wrote: 'Francis Ouimet became a national hero. To the public he was the all-American boy, the young man from a family of modest means who had entered a field dominated by professionals and amateurs of wealth and social position and had shown he could play the game better than any of them. He was an unassuming hero, partly because of his solid upbringing.' A year later Ouimet won the US Amateur title, as he would again 17 years later, and in 1951 became the first overseas captain of the Royal and Ancient.

JIM BARNES

Born April 8, 1886, Lelant, Cornwall;
died March 25, 1966, East Orange, New Jersey
USPGA champion 1916 and '19;
US Open champion 1921; Open champion 1925

Just as American amateur golf was reaching its peak – Bobby Jones was still to come – came the founding of the Professional Golfers' Association of America in New York in 1916, some 15 years after the British original. One of the key people behind the organisation was businessman Rodman Wanamaker, whose huge trophy is awarded to the winner of the PGA Championship (distinguished here as the USPGA). The event was played as matchplay for its first 39 editions and although the designation of 'major' evolved later, it was considered a significant tournament alongside the US Open. The first champion was Jim Barnes in 1916 and he retained the title three years later when the tournament resumed after the First World War.

Barnes was another naturalised American. He was from Cornwall and was an assistant professional at West Cornwall before moving to San Francisco at the age of 19. He was known as 'Long Jim' since, at six foot, four inches, he was the first tall man to become successful in the game. No one above six foot had previously survived at the top of the game but Barnes proved there was no inherent disadvantage in being so tall. He even played well in the wind, having learnt to play on the links of Cornwall.

His greatest achievement was winning the US Open in 1921 at Columbia, where he led from start to finish and won by nine strokes from Walter Hagen and Fred McLeod. Barnes might have won more titles but for Hagen, who beat him in the final of the USPGA in 1921 and '24. Barnes was also runner-up to Hagen in the 1922 Open at Royal St. George's but three years later Barnes won the claret jug having started the final round five strokes behind Macdonald Smith. Another of the Carnoustie brothers, Smith was an early contender for the best player never to win a major, finishing within three strokes of the champion on nine occasions. In the last

Open to be played at Prestwick, the large gallery so overwhelmed the course that Smith, needing to score a 78 to win, could only return an 82. Barnes had become the second player, after Hagen, to win all three of what we now call major championships prior to the creation of the Masters.

Barnes was a quiet, modest man and always proud of his English roots. Prior to the Sandwich Open in 1922, he played a round at neighbouring Prince's and was followed throughout by Laddie Lucas, the six-year-old son of the club's secretary. After the round, Barnes gave Laddie two dozen brand new golf balls and said he could keep any that he drove into the fairway from the first tee. Despite a strong crosswind, Lucas hit all 24 onto the fairway and the supply lasted him over two years. In the Second World War, Lucas was a renowned fighter pilot and once had to crash land on Prince's, which had been taken over by the military. When he ended up in a bunker at the ninth, he said: 'Never could hit that fairway.'

GEORGE DUNCAN

Born September 16, 1883, Methlick, Aberdeenshire;
died January 15, 1964, Leeds, Yorkshire
Open champion 1920

Like Ted Ray, George Duncan was a successor to the Great Triumvirate and came to prominence before the First World War. He claimed the claret jug in the first post-War Open but golf had changed. The Americans were now about to dominate. Following Duncan's win in 1920, 11 of the next 13 Opens were won by visitors from across the Atlantic. Only Arthur Havers in 1923 bucked the trend as a home-based champion.

Instead of Duncan, it might have been Abe Mitchell in 1920. Mitchell led by six strokes after the first two rounds at Deal, with Duncan 13 behind. No one else has ever recovered from such a position to win the Open. Feeling his driving had let him down

Jim Barnes

GEORGE DUNCAN

after twin rounds of 80, Duncan visited the exhibition tent and bought a new driver. The transformation was complete as the next day he returned rounds of 71 and 72 to beat Sandy Herd by two strokes. Mitchell had collapsed in the third round, an 84 eating up his advantage and a 76 in the last round dropping him to fourth place. Mitchell was thought one of the best British players never to win the Open but, as the personal coach of St. Albans seed merchant Samuel Ryder, he played a crucial part in the establishment of a soon-to-be regular transatlantic match that would become the Ryder Cup.

Duncan was the son of an Aberdeenshire village policeman and apprenticed as a carpenter before turning professional at 17. His key characteristic can be guessed from the title of his autobiography, *Golf at the Gallop*. Never the most secure putter, his policy was: 'If you are going to miss 'em, miss 'em quick.' James Braid, however, wrote: 'I cannot make him out; he plays so fast that he looks like he doesn't care, but I suppose it must be his way.'

Two years after his Open win, Duncan had a chance at Sandwich to tie Walter Hagen, whose clubhouse target was considered so secure that telegrams had been sent to London proclaiming a new champion. But Duncan, still out on the course, sent approach shot after approach shot rifling at the flags, until the last where he needed a four to force a playoff. His second shot, struck possibly too well in that it did not fade back from the left, found a dip to the left of the green. In the blink of an eye that it took to play his chip, the ball returned to his feet and he took a five. Duncan's Hollow, as it became known, was also visited in 1985 by Sandy Lyle, who also fluffed his chip but found a five was still good enough to win. Duncan had some revenge in 1929, in the first Ryder Cup on home soil, when the Scot trounced Hagen, his opposite number as captain, 10 and 8.

In 1921 Jock Hutchinson, St. Andrews born and bred but, like Jim Barnes, a naturalised American, won the Open on the Old Course but his provenance, Bernard Darwin wrote, 'did not seem so much comfort in practice as in theory.' America was about to unleash its own triumvirate of stars: Hagen, Gene Sarazen and Bobby Jones.

WALTER HAGEN

Born December 21, 1892 Rochester, New York;
died October 5, 1969, Traverse City, Michigan
US Open champion 1914 and '19;
USPGA champion 1921, '24, '25, '26 and '27;
Open champion 1922, '24, '28 and '29

As with Arnold Palmer in the Swinging Sixties and Seve Ballesteros in Europe in the Eighties, so Walter Hagen in the Roaring Twenties was the perfect golfer at the right time. He was a flamboyant showman who proved golf could provide the most exciting entertainment. Gene Sarazen said about Hagen what others later would say of Palmer and Ballesteros: 'All the professionals who have a chance to go after the big money should say a silent thanks to Walter each time they stretch a cheque between their fingers. It was Walter who made professional golf what it is.'

There were the stories of taking time to 'smell the roses', of being out all night and turning up at the course in a tuxedo, and of enquiring of his opponents: 'So which one of you is going to finish second?' Herb Warren Wind said he broke 'eleven of the Ten Commandments and kept on going.' At the 1920 Open at Deal, told he could not enter the clubhouse, he merely dined and changed his shoes in his Austin-Daimler parked by the front door.

A well-built man who once toyed with the idea of becoming a baseball player, Hagen had an inconsistent, swaying swing which produced many a horrendous shot. He accepted wherever he ended up and got on with the recovery. From 100 yards and in, he was superb. He pitched brilliantly, he was precise from sand long before the sand wedge was invented and he was an inspired putter.

It added up to an alluring package. 'Anyone who knew Hagen,' wrote Henry Longhurst, 'would probably go further to see him play again in his prime than anyone else in the world.' Then there were the clothes. At the time when most pros were still dressing in sack coats and brogues, Hagen wore silk shirts, florid cravats, alpaca sweaters, screaming argyles and black-and-white shoes he had custom-made at a $100 a pair, reported Charles Price.

WALTER HAGEN

Hagen was the son of a blacksmith from Rochester, New York, where he became one of the first American-born club professionals. After winning his second US Open in 1919, he gave up his then position at Oakland Hills to become 'unattached', a full-time tournament professional, a modern Young Tom Morris. 'The Haig', or 'Sir Walter', hired a manager and set up exhibition tours which, over the years, took him around the globe.

But as Al Laney wrote, 'All of us who wrote golf in Hagen's day made too much of his flamboyant showmanship and not nearly enough of his golf.' His total of 11 major titles has only been surpassed by Jack Nicklaus and Tiger Woods. He won four Opens out of six, and, at matchplay, five USPGAs out of six, finishing runner-up the other year after an epic final against Sarazen.

Facing Hagen head-to-head was virtually impossible. Bernard Darwin wrote: 'His demeanour to his opponents, though entirely correct, had yet a certain suppressed truculence; he exhibited so supreme a confidence that they could not get it out of their minds and could not live against it.' Bobby Jones was one of the few to withstand the glare. 'I love to play with Walter,' he said. 'He goes along chin up, smiling away; never grousing about his luck, playing the ball as he finds it. He can come nearer beating the luck itself than anybody I know.'

GENE SARAZEN

Born February 27, 1902, Harrison, New York;
died May 13, 1999, Naples, Florida
US Open champion 1922 and '32; USPGA champion 1922, '23
and '33; Open champion 1932; Masters champion 1935

Who invented the sand wedge? Who was the only player to beat Walter Hagen in six years at the USPGA? Who was a contemporary of Bobby Jones but won first and kept playing longer? Who won the only Open at Prince's? Who was the first to win all four major championships? Who hit the 'shot heard around the world'? Who starred in a film with Buster Keaton? Who was chris-

tened Eugenio Saraceni but changed his name aged 17 because he did not want to sound like a violinist? The answer is Gene Sarazen.

The son of an Italian immigrant carpenter, Sarazen started caddying at the age of ten. He almost died of pneumonia while working as an apprentice to his father – the same illness finally claimed him aged 97 – and after weeks in hospital, his doctors recommended an outdoor lifestyle. Golf it was, then. He won the 1922 US Open aged 20 and then added the USPGA title. Walter Hagen had won the Open and the two played a 72-hole match for the 'world championship' which the younger Sarazen won. Hagen had not played in the USPGA, even though he had won in 1921, but the two met in the final in 1923, with Sarazen winning at the 38th hole – Hagen went on to win the next four USPGAs.

Sarazen, meanwhile, became briefly distracted by Hollywood, where he dabbled in movies. As well as becoming a more cautious player, 'The Squire' – he lived on a farm for much of his life – also did something about his poor bunker play. By building up the flange of his wedge with solder, Sarazen invented the modern sand wedge, designed to glide through the sand when hitting behind the ball and exploding both sand and ball safely out of the trap. The next summer he returned to England and won the 1932 Open at Prince's, the neighbouring links to Royal St. George's.

His association with the Open had started in 1923 at Troon when, even as a two-time major winner, he failed to qualify, and finished at the same venue in 1973, where he holed in one with a five-iron at the Postage Stamp (the eighth hole). The next day he holed out of a bunker for a two.

Sarazen, always genial and dressed in plus-fours, missed the inaugural Masters in 1934 at Bobby Jones' recently completed Augusta National course, but the following year he hit the 'shot heard around the world' when a four-wood approach at the 15th went in the hole for an albatross, or double eagle as the Americans put it. At a stroke he had wiped out a three-shot deficit and he went on to beat Craig Wood in a playoff. Jones's new tournament never looked back. 'Sarazen has always been the impatient player who went for everything in the hope of feeling the timely touch of inspiration,' wrote Jones. 'When he is right in the mood, he is probably the greatest scorer in the game, possibly that the game has ever seen.'

Yet in 1934 on a world exhibition tour, Sarazen stopped in Fiji on his way to Australia and was practising at Suva when some local caddies, marvelling at his great shots, asked who he was. 'Don't you know who I am? My name is Gene Sarazen,' he said. The reply came: 'We no hear of Mister Sarazen, but we hear of Mister Jones.'

BOBBY JONES

Born March 17, 1902, Atlanta, Georgia;
died December 18, 1971, Atlanta, Georgia
US Open champion 1923, '26, '29 and '30;
US Amateur champion 1924, '25, '27, '28 and '30;
Open champion 1926, '27 and '30;
Amateur champion 1930

B obby Jones was more than a golfer, he was a hero in an era when the word meant something. In the eight seasons between 1923 and 1930, Jones entered 21 national championships and won 13 of them. In that time, the two greatest professionals of the time, Walter Hagen and Gene Sarazen, never won when Jones was in the field. As an amateur, Jones's 'majors' consisted of the Open and Amateur championships of America and Britain. In 1930, he won all four of them, what came to be known as the Grand Slam. Jones was honoured with two tickertape parades in New York that summer. He was aged 28 and, after a few months of consideration, promptly retired from competitive golf. He went out at the top, a peak no one has since come close to scaling.

Jones grew up in Atlanta and was a natural from the beginning, learning the fundamentals from East Lake's Scottish professional, Stewart Maiden. Bernard Darwin wrote: 'Harry Vardon and Bobby Jones combined exquisiteness of art with utterly relentless precision in a way not given to any other golfer.' Darwin also described Jones's swing: 'I can remember the precise spot at Hoylake where I first saw

BOBBY JONES

the swing soon to be familiar in the imagination of the whole golfing world; so swift in that it occupied so little time, with no suspicion of waggle, and yet so leisurely in its drowsy grace, so lithe and so smooth.' Here was a thing of beauty to add to the dashing manner he played the game. 'I can play this game only one way,' he said, 'I must play every shot for all there is in it. I can't play safe.'

He won four US Opens, was runner-up four times and never worse than 11th in 11 appearances. He won the US Amateur five times, still a record. He won three of the four Opens he played, including in 1927 at St. Andrews, a course that had got the better of him six years earlier. He won 58 of 69 matches in the US and British Amateurs. He won the latter only once, at St. Andrews, but it was the start of the Slam. He then won the Open at Hoylake and sailed back to New York. The US Open followed at Interlachen and then the US Amateur at Merion. After winning the final, such was the delirium of the gallery on the way back to the clubhouse the *New York Times* reported: 'It was the most triumphant journey that any man ever travelled in sport.'

With degrees in engineering, literature and law from Georgia Tech and Harvard, he went into business and the law on his retirement, and also created the glory that is Augusta National and set up the Masters from 1934, when a few friends came to honour the Emperor. They still do.

In 1958 Jones followed Benjamin Franklin as the only Americans to be given the freedom of the Royal Burgh of St. Andrews. It was an intensely emotional day. 'If I could take out of my life everything but my experiences in St. Andrews, I would still have led a rich, full life,' he said.

Jones was quiet and genuinely modest about his achievements. He called penalty strokes on himself and was surprised at the reaction. 'You might as well praise a man for not robbing a bank,' he said. For the last 23 years of his life he became increasingly incapacitated due to syringomyelia, a disease of the spinal column. Bitter at first, he 'decided I'd just do the very best I could'. Ben Hogan said of Jones: 'The man was sick so long and fought it so successfully, I think we've finally discovered the secret of his success. It was the strength of his mind.'

CECIL LEITCH

Born April 13, 1891, Silloth, Cumbria;
died September 16, 1977 (location unconfirmed)
British Ladies Amateur champion 1914, '20, '21 and '26

B obby Jones said the finest player he had ever seen was Joyce
Wethered, whose battles with Cecil Leitch irreversibly advanced
both the standard and the popularity of the women's game. Their
rivalry became front-page news and each defined the other's greatness. Wethered could not become the queen without dethroning
Charlotte Cecilia Pitcairn Leitch, known to all as Cecil.

Leitch was the daughter of Silloth's doctor. The local golf club,
opened by the North British Railway Company a year after her birth,
became the playground for Leitch and her sisters, two of whom also
earned international honours. In 1908 she caused a stir by reaching
the semi-finals of the British Ladies Amateur Championship at the
age of 17 and two years later she won a 72-hole challenge match
against the mighty Harold Hilton. She received a stroke every other
hole but the important thing was the way she finished: from five-
down with 15 to play she stormed to a 2 and 1 victory.

She was clearly a force of nature. Bernard Darwin wrote: 'I have
a vision of her with her familiar bandeau on her head and some sort
of handkerchief knotted round her neck, affronting the tempest,
revelling in her defiance of it. The wide stance, the little duck of the
right knee, the follow-through that sends the club through low as if
boring its way through the wind. Think of Madame Defarge leading
the women of St. Antoine against the Bastille.'

Hitting the ball long and straight, as the links at Silloth demand,
Leitch soon became the best woman player, winning the first of five
French titles in 1912. The second arrived two years later when she
did the double of the English and British titles. Her four British titles
is a record shared by Wethered, while she won the Canadian title in
1921 by claiming the final 17 and 15 – she was 14 up at lunch and
needed only three more holes in the afternoon.

Her second English title came after the War in 1919 but the following year she ran into Wethered at Sheringham and never won the

CECIL LEITCH

English again. Leitch did have revenge in 1921, beating Wethered in the final of both the French and the British, but lost in the final of the latter to Wethered in both 1922 and '25. Her rival was the first to acknowledge how Leitch was inspired on the big occasion. 'The vitality of her character was capable of electrifying the whole atmosphere,' Wethered said.

The 1925 final at Troon proved a famous climax to their epic encounters. Henry Longhurst wrote, 'there are many who say that the concluding stages were the greatest match they have ever seen.' Three-up earlier in the day, Leitch had to win the last two holes to force extra time and Wethered only won at the 37th. Darwin, who was present, thought Leitch, 'rather than her conqueror, was the heroine of the day. Everyone who saw that match will always wish that there could for that year have been two queens on twin thrones of exactly equal splendour.'

JOYCE WETHERED

Born November 17, 1901, Surrey;
died November 18, 1997, Tiverton, Devon
British Ladies Amateur champion
1922, '24, '25 and '29

Acclaimed as the supreme woman golfer of her time, the parallels between Joyce Wethered and Bobby Jones are striking. Both retired at a relatively young age from championship golf after compiling dominating records. Wethered played in five English Ladies Championships and won all five. In the British Ladies she won four times at six attempts, being a finalist and a semi-finalist on the other occasions. Yet she was also a quiet, modest person. In the English final at Sheringham, Norfolk, in 1920 she faced a putt to win when a train steamed past. Asked later about the distraction, she exclaimed, 'What train?' Wethered later said: 'Possibly I was so bewildered at the thought of what I was doing that if the very heavens had fallen, I should not have noticed.'

Joyce Wethered

Jones played with Wethered at St. Andrews in 1930, off the back tees in a decent breeze. She scored a 75. 'I have not played golf with anyone, man or woman, amateur or professional, who made me feel so utterly outclassed,' said Jones. 'It was not so much the score she made as the way she made it. It was impossible to expect that Miss Wethered would ever miss a shot – and she never did.'

Concentration and nerve were backed up by fine putting, a good short game and a long game that produced, Sir Henry Cotton reckoned, shots as straight as only Harry Vardon could have conjured up. She was said to be as accurate with her woods as others were with a wedge. Balance was the key to her swing. 'I wonder if anyone who watched her can honestly recollect a single stroke during any period of which she was not in perfect equilibrium?' asked noted golf writer Henry Longhurst.

Born into a golfing family in Surrey, growing up near the West Surrey course, Joyce was pushed on by her golf-mad brother Roger, an Amateur champion himself and the runner-up in the 1921 Open. Aged just 18, and playing to keep a friend company, Joyce won the English title in 1920 by beating her great rival Cecil Leitch in the final, a shock to both of them. Not only did Joyce overcome a huge deficit but also whooping cough, which sidelined her for the next three months.

Perhaps it was an early manifestation of what championship golf took out of her, and after the epic final of the British in 1925 against Leitch she withdrew until tempted back for the British in 1929 only because it was at St. Andrews. Another classic final ensued, this time against the great American Glenna Collett. Five-down after 11 holes, Wethered produced one more mighty comeback and promptly retired again. There was an exhibition tour in America in 1935 and she also continued to play in the Worplesdon Mixed Foursomes, which she won eight times with seven different partners. Bernard Darwin was 'one of that fortunate body of men who have been hauled through to victory by the scruffs of their necks by Miss Joyce Wethered.'

In 1937 she married Sir John Heathcote-Amory, and moved to Tiverton, in Devon. Her garden became her pride and joy and it was taken over by the National Trust in 1972 when her husband died. She lived on until the day after her 96th birthday.

GLENNA COLLETT VARE

Born June 20, 1903, New Haven, Connecticut;
died February 3, 1989, Gulfstream, Florida
US Women's Amateur champion 1922, '25, '28, '29, '30 and '35

Glenna Collett, later known by her married name of Vare, was the undisputed queen of American golf in the 1920s and '30s. She won the US Women's Amateur title six times between 1922 and '35 and was runner-up twice. She won two other prime US amateur competitions, the North and South, and the Eastern, six times each, as well as the Canadian title twice and the French in 1925. But the British title always eluded her.

Twice she lost to Joyce Wethered, in the semi-finals in 1925 and in the final in 1929. In the latter, Collett's brilliance over the opening holes meant she went to the turn of the Old Course in 34 and was five-up after 11 holes. Only Wethered's very best over the rest of the match prevented a first American victory in the championship. Collett was also denied in the final the following year, by the 19-year-old Diana Fishwick, later mother of television commentator Bruce Critchley.

'If she is finding her true form, then there is little hope, except by miracle, of surviving,' wrote Wethered, one of the few capable of coming up with the necessary miracle. In 1924 Collett won 59 out of 60 matches, only losing in the semi-finals of the US Amateur at the 19th hole. In the Curtis Cup – the match between the women amateurs of America and Britain and Ireland in which she played between 1932 and '48 – her record was won four, halved two and lost one. Her matchplay attributes she described as: 'love of combat, serenity of mind and fearlessness.'

Learning her golf from former US Open champion Alex Smith, Collett was the first American woman to attack the ball, and drives of over 300 yards were not unknown. Enid Wilson, a Curtis Cup opponent, wrote: 'Her vigorous game set up an entirely fresh standard for her countrywomen, and the young up-and-coming golfers in the 1930s were inspired by her example.' One such was Patty Berg, who was 17 when she lost to the 32-year-old mother-of-two in the

Glenna Collett Vare

1935 final of the US Amateur. Berg became a founder member of the LPGA, which annually awards the Vare Trophy for the season's best scoring average.

Wethered and Collett were firm friends despite being enemies on the course. When Wethered undertook a tour in America in 1935, she played several matches with Collett. 'Her charm to my mind as a golfer and a companion lies in a freedom of spirit which does not make her feel that success is everything in the world,' said Wethered.

Collett said of Wethered: 'She is as near perfection as I ever dreamed of being when I sat in a deep-seated rocker on the front porch in the cool summer evening years ago and dreamed my best dreams.'

Nelson, Hogan, Snead and the Babe
1930–1950

Following on from the reign of Bobby Jones, American domination of the game continued apace. Against this backdrop, Henry Cotton was a rare British hero and his Open victories were joyously celebrated. His 65 at Sandwich in 1934 was a record that lasted for 43 years. But this era is really defined by three American greats, Byron Nelson, Ben Hogan and Sam Snead. Unlike Hogan and Snead, Nelson never won the Open, but his accuracy and control were astonishing given the baked-out courses of the time. He produced one of the game's great achievements when he won 11 tournaments in a row, and 18 in all, in 1945.

Nelson retired early but Hogan was only just figuring out how to win. His dominance, and the level that American golf had reached, were exemplified in 1953 when he won all three of the majors he played in, including the Open at Carnoustie. Snead had a long and successful career, still topping the list of PGA Tour victories today, but never quite managed to capture the US Open. Meanwhile, as women's professional golf really got going, its star was Babe Zaharias, an all-round athletic goddess who brought glamour to the game while also showing that women golfers could hit the ball with tremendous power.

Tommy Armour

TOMMY ARMOUR

Born September 24, 1895, Edinburgh;
died September 11, 1968, Larchmont, New York
US Open champion 1927; USPGA champion 1930;
Open champion 1931

Tommy Armour, born in Edinburgh and educated at Fettes College and Edinburgh University, remains the last Scottish-born player to win the US Open and the USPGA – and was the last to win the Open before Sandy Lyle 54 years later, and the last to do so in Scotland until Paul Lawrie in 1999. As a naturalised American who had played for Britain as an amateur and for his adopted country as a professional, the 'Silver Scot' was the last of a kind.

Yet he came to the game relatively late, since first came the First World War in which he lost the sight of an eye when his tank was hit by artillery. It was also said that he strangled a German soldier with his bare hands.

He was already a French Amateur champion when he went to America and then he turned professional in 1924. Within seven years he had become the third player to win all three of the major championships. Two of those victories came at two of the hardest golf courses then seen, in Oakmont and Carnoustie. The tougher it was, the more Armour enjoyed it. At Oakmont in 1927, he birdied the last to tie Harry 'Lighthorse' Cooper and then won a playoff the next day. In 1930 he won the one major which Bobby Jones could not enter, the USPGA, where he beat Gene Sarazen by one-hole in the final. Then, a year later, he won the title he really cherished, the Open at Carnoustie with a final round of 71, six better than the third-round leader Jose Jurado, of Argentina.

Some journalists, such as Bernard Darwin, marvelled at the strike Armour achieved with his iron shots, while others thought him an even better driver. His weakness was his putting, which developed into the 'yips'. But when he was in contention, he was tough to beat, as golf writer Herb Warren Wind described in *The Story of American Golf*: 'Whenever the Silver Scot played himself into a contending position, he always seemed to have that extra something that was the difference between barely losing and barely winning. He was singularly unaffected by the pressure of the last stretch. His hands were hot but his head was cool.'

Armour himself said: 'It is not solely the capacity to make great shots that makes champions, but the essential quality of making very few bad shots.' Good or bad, Armour, an inveterate waggler, certainly took his time over his shots, enquiring: 'Whoever said golf was supposed to be played fast?'

After his playing career, he became a noted, and well-remunerated, teacher, often based at Winged Foot in the summer and Boca Raton in Florida in the winter. He wrote two well-received books. The first, *How to Play Your Best Golf All the Time*, was subtitled: 'Hit the hell out of the ball with your right hand.' His other tome was *A Round of Golf with Tommy Armour*. Charles Price summed him up as having 'a dash of indifference, a touch of class, and a bit of majesty.'

SIR HENRY COTTON

Born January 26, 1907, Holmes Chapel;
died December 22, 1987, London
Open champion 1934, '37 and '48

Henry Cotton was simply 'Maestro'. It had been a decade since the last home winner of the Open and there had only been two since the War. Britain needed a new golfing hero and Cotton, the only multiple Open champion between the Great Triumvirate and Nick Faldo, fitted the bill.

Growing up in London and attending a public school, he might have been a classy amateur and 'something in the city'. But while still a teenager he wanted to become a professional and JH Taylor, whom his father consulted, provided encouragement. He worked at a number of clubs but also practised for long, blister-inducing hours, including it was said, by moonlight at Rye. An early trip to America proved beneficial to his game and his image, as he was much taken with the Walter Hagen approach that 'to be a champion, you must act like one'.

SIR HENRY COTTON

Only the best hotels would do, and in a long career he spent time at Royal Waterloo in Brussels, in the south of France (with a golf school in Monte Carlo) and, once his playing days were over, at Penina, in the Algarve, where he designed the course. He performed exhibitions in music halls, including the London Palladium, and mixed easily with everyone he met. He helped set up the Golf Foundation, wrote ten books and became the first golfer to be knighted for his services to the game. He accepted the title but the official announcement did not come until after his death at the age of 80. Throughout he had the loyal support of his Argentinian-born wife 'Toots'.

According to Henry Longhurst, there was a 'magnetism about Cotton in Open championships which to me has never quite been equalled'. At Sandwich in 1934 he opened with a 67 and then added a record 65, with birdies at the last two holes. It was a score celebrated by the famous 'Dunlop 65' ball and was not beaten at the Open until 1977. Twelve shots ahead going into the final round, Cotton found his game had deserted him and 'played in a cold sweat'. But a 79 still did the job and he was hailed a hero. Later that night at his hotel, he handed the trophy to Harry Vardon, who had not been well enough to watch the golf that day. 'There were tears glistening in both our eyes,' Cotton said.

Three years later at Carnoustie, against the might of the US Ryder Cup team, Cotton won again, with a 71 in the final round amid heavy rain, which to many observers was one of the best rounds ever played. Another majestic effort was the 66 he scored in the second round of the 1948 Open at Muirfield in front of King George VI; he went on to his third title at the age of 41. But for the War, how many more might there have been?

Longhurst wrote: 'We often used to challenge him to take his driver from a bad lie on the fairway, simply for the aesthetic pleasure of seeing the ball fly away as though fired from a rifle. I remember once seeing him knock a shooting stick out of the ground with a one-iron at a range of 20 yards. We christened him the "Maestro", and he deserved it.'

LAWSON LITTLE

Born June 23, 1910, Newport, Rhode Island;
died February 1, 1968, Monterey, California
Amateur champion 1934 and '35; US Amateur champion 1934
and '35; US Open champion 1940

Lawson Little was the man who beat the man who beat Bobby Jones. He then went on to outdo Jones by winning the Amateur Championship of Britain and America in the same year for two years running. The 'Little Slam' meant winning 31 consecutive matches and most of them were not even close. Only three times was he taken the distance and only once was he forced into extra holes.

Little was the son of a doctor who was a colonel in the US Army, which meant a nomadic childhood until the family settled in Northern California. In 1929 he entered the US Amateur at Pebble Beach. This was the year the unthinkable happened and Jones lost in the first round to Johnny Goodman. But Goodman's fortune was short-lived as he lost to the 19-year-old Little in the afternoon. The following year Little enrolled at Stanford, as did Tom Watson and Tiger Woods decades later, and in 1933 got to the semi-finals of the US Amateur, which earned him a place on the 1934 Walker Cup team at St. Andrews.

The Scottish galleries would have heard of Goodman, the last amateur to win a major when he claimed the 1933 US Open, but they were soon to find out about Little. He and Goodman won their foursomes against the established pairing of Roger Wethered and Cyril Tolley 8 and 6 before Little beat Tolley 6 and 5 in the singles. Moving to Prestwick, Little swept all before him, eventually thrashing James Wallace in the final 14 and 13 – having taken 82 strokes for the 23 holes played. Bernard Darwin said it was 'one of the most terrific exhibitions in all golfing history'. Little returned home and won the US Amateur before repeating the feat the following year.

Bullnecked and barrel-chested, Little gave the ball a great thump with a draw and then relied on his touch around the greens and precise putting. He was helped with his pitching by carrying seven or more wedges. The estimates of how many clubs he sometimes

LAWSON
LITTLE

carried ranges from 23 to 26 to 31. In 1938 the USGA imposed the current limit of 14 clubs, now the norm worldwide. His Army background contributed to his thorough preparations. He said: 'I became saturated with the military idea that the more a soldier knows about the ground he fights upon, the better his chances for victory. Very well, why not regard a golf course as a personal battleground? Whenever I go into competition, my first concern is the battlefield. Or, to be more precise, the 18 battlefields.'

Little turned professional and won the Canadian Open but he only won eight times on the USPGA Tour, including a playoff victory over Gene Sarazen at the 1940 US Open. But his interest in golf waned after the War, and the promise of his professional career never lived up to the brilliance of his amateur achievements. He died aged 57 having had heart problems for some years and brain surgery in 1963.

BYRON NELSON

Born February 4, 1912, Waxahachie, Texas;
died September 26, 2006, Roanoke, Texas
Masters champion 1937 and '42; US Open champion 1939;
USPGA champion 1940 and '45

Golf's next great trio was Byron Nelson, Sam Snead and Ben Hogan, all born within six months of each other. Nelson and Hogan were both Texans and competed in the final of the caddies' competition at Glen Garden in 1927. Nelson won narrowly and was the first to achieve greatness; Hogan only did after Nelson retired at the age of 34. Like Bobby Jones, Nelson had done everything he wished to do on the golf course. Like Jones, he had one of the greatest single seasons the game has seen. In 1945, Nelson created 'The Streak', winning 11 consecutive events on the USPGA Tour. The record at the time was four; only Hogan and Tiger Woods, with six each, have got more than halfway. Nelson won 18 events in all that year and finished second seven times.

Nelson was perhaps the first player to recognise that the big muscles must play the most important role in the swing. Not for him a wristy flick. 'Nobody kept the ball on the clubface longer through impact,' Ken Venturi told *Golf Digest*. 'He could hook and fade it easily, but Byron could hit the ball dead straight on demand. That's the hardest thing in golf.' The USGA's mechanical swing device for testing clubs and balls was named 'Iron Byron' in his honour.

At the 1939 US Open, Nelson hit the flagstick six times in the regulation 72 holes, each time with a different club: wedge, nine, six, four, one-iron and driver. During the playoff he holed a one-iron for an eagle two. He had already won the Masters in 1937, a two at the 12th and a three at the 13th making up six strokes on leader Ralph Guldahl. OB Keeler named him 'Lord Byron' that day.

In 1942, Nelson and Hogan were in a playoff for the Masters and Nelson played eight holes from the sixth in six under. He needed to – Hogan was only beaten by a stroke in one of the all-time memorable Augusta contests. In 1944 he won eight times but worried he had thrown away shots due to poor chipping and blips in concentration – the latter caused simply by playing too well! Nelson, the head pro at Inverness in Toledo up to 1944, upped his game and, despite claims to the contrary, faced all the top names of the time. 'I don't care if he was playing against orang-utans,' said Jackie Burke. 'Winning 11 straight is amazing.'

Another streak that no longer stands – beaten by Woods – is Nelson's record of 113 consecutive times 'in the money'. But in those days, only the top 15, perhaps 20, got paid, so it, too, is an amazing feat. After the 1946 season, Nelson had enough money to buy a ranch in Roanoke, Texas, where he and his wife Louise retired. 'I finally had to admit I'd accomplished everything I'd set out to do in golf,' he said. 'I wasn't sick. I wasn't scared of the pressure like some speculated. I was just tired and I'd achieved my goal. Once we'd given them the money and signed the papers and the ranch was ours, nothing else mattered.'

Nelson remained the finest gentleman in the game. He became a television commentator and mentored Venturi and Tom Watson, as well as hosting the old Dallas Open when it was named after him.

BYRON NELSON

Playing exhibitions with Venturi, he would always ask the course record and who held it. If it was the host pro, they would never break it. 'He lives here, we're only visiting,' Nelson said.

BEN HOGAN

Born August 13, 1912, Stephenville, Texas;
died July 29, 1997, Forth Worth, Texas
USPGA champion 1946 and '48;
US Open champion 1948, '50, '51 and '53;
Masters champion 1951 and '53;
Open champion 1953

The year after Byron Nelson won 18 times, Ben Hogan won 13 times. While Nelson's best golf came during the War, Hogan's came after it. He needed patience but had it in spades. He was, after all, the man who 'dug it out of the dirt'. Plagued by a hook at first, he refined and refined his swing, until a fade was perfected. 'I always outworked everybody,' he said. 'Work never bothered me like it bothers some people.' He was the first to practise after a round, especially his best rounds. He simply kept getting better – until he was the best. There was talk of a secret formula he had discovered. If so, he wasn't telling. His words were sparingly issued but he did bequeath the golfing world *The Modern Fundamentals of Golf*, his best-selling instruction tome.

Hogan had to scrap for everything in his life, at times barely being able to stay out on tour. But from his first major win at the 1946 USPGA, he won nine times in 16 appearances. It might never have got that far because in February 1949, on a foggy night, his car collided with a Greyhound bus. By throwing himself in front of his wife, Valerie, in the passenger seat, he saved both her life and his. He broke a collarbone, a rib, his pelvis and an ankle. A blood clot developed and almost killed him again. It was a year before he could return to competition, and winning the US Open at Merion in 1950 was the moment he most cherished.

From Merion, to Carnoustie in 1953, he won six majors in eight appearances. In 1951, he won a third US Open in three appearances, on an Oakland Hills course that was so hard, only Hogan could handle it. 'I'm glad I brought this course, this monster, to its knees,' he said.

In 1953, a year he owns in the same way as 1930 belongs to Bobby Jones, he played six tournaments and won five of them. Three were majors, the Masters by five strokes, the US Open by six and the Open by four – it would have been more but he hardly holed a putt all week. It was Hogan's only appearance in Scotland and the man in the white cap, cigarette to hand, that glaring stare permanently in place, was adored by the local golfers, who were said to refer to him as the 'Wee Ice Mon' for his nerve under pressure.

Gene Sarazen said no one 'covered the flag' like Hogan, Jack Nicklaus that he was the greatest ever shot-maker. Pat Ward-Thomas wrote: 'There is no doubt that Hogan came closer than anyone to eliminating the human element from golf. The swing he created was not beautiful. The tempo was fastish; it was remote from the lazy effortless grace of Jones or Snead, but there was about it a wonderful sense of precision, like an instrument of flawless tempered steel. He seemed immune to the pressures that destroy other golfers.'

Hogan said: 'I think anyone can do anything he wants to do if he wants to study and work hard enough. I have got great satisfaction, as much as or more than anybody, in learning how to swing a golf club. There's nine jillion things to learn. But what lay behind my new confidence after 1946 was that I stopped trying to do a great many difficult things perfectly because it had become clear in my mind that this ambitious overthoroughness was neither possible nor advisable or even necessary. All you needed to groove were the fundamental movements – and there aren't so many of them.'

Ben Hogan

SAM SNEAD

Born May 27, 1912, Ashwood, Virginia;
died May 23, 2002, Hot Springs, Virginia
USPGA champion 1942, '49 and '51; Open champion 1946;
Masters champion 1949, '52 and '54

'The only things I fear in golf,' Sam Snead said, 'are lightning, a downhill putt and Ben Hogan.' However, Snead did stop Hogan claiming a fourth major in a row by winning an 18-hole playoff for the 1954 Masters. It was his seventh major victory, and his best, as well as his third green jacket – he had been the first to receive the famous garment when the tradition began in 1949.

When it came to the US Open, however, Snead never managed a victory. Four times he was a runner-up, including in 1947 when he was two ahead with three to play in a playoff against Lew Worsham but lost by three-putting at the last. Earlier, he had taken an eight at the 72nd hole in 1939, when a par would have put him in a playoff, and in 1940 he took an 81 in the final round when in contention. One year at a US Open, he said he was 'so tight you couldn' a' drove flax seed down my throat with a knot maul.'

Snead hailed from the Blue Ridge Mountains in Virginia and first played golf amid the valley pastures by whittling the branch of a maple tree into a club. He played barefoot, but then from May to October no boy wore shoes in those parts. He started caddying at a local course, became an assistant and was then invited to play at the posh hotel the other side of the mountain, The Greenbrier in White Sulphur Springs. It was his break, and he was based at the resort evermore, eventually becoming the first player to score a 59.

Snead, or 'Slammin' Sam', was the most athletic male golfer of the 20th century. He could kick his foot above his head and his swing was just a thing of beauty, bringing 'tears of joy to the eyes,' wrote Bernard Darwin. Ted Williams, the great baseball player and a friend of Snead, said: 'Everybody who ever saw him swing a golf club knew they'd seen something to remember. Terrifically built with those shoulders, no hips, power in those legs. Sammy was strong and he was fluid.'

Sam Snead

'He has always been a long driver,' wrote Henry Longhurst, 'but he does not give the impression of hitting it hard.' Peter Alliss said: 'If anyone ever played golf in a more elegant way than Sam, I'd like to know who it was. He had everything: rhythm, balance, power, touch, skill, the most wonderful walk (almost to rival Sean Connery) and a wicked sense of humour, even if at times it might have been considered rather "bawdy".'

Snead journeyed to St. Andrews in 1946 and on the train into the town he thought he saw an abandoned golf course. It was the Old Course. He won despite strong winds in the final round but never contemplated returning to defend the title having lost money on the trip. No one has yet won more than Snead's 82 PGA Tour titles, collected between 1936 and '65. There were countless other unofficial victories but he said he would give away half of them all just for a US Open. 'Hardly anyone has meant so much to the Open,' wrote Robert Sommers of America's national championship, 'as Snead, and certainly no one else captured – and broke – so many hearts.'

JIMMY DEMARET

Born May 24, 1910, Houston, Texas;
died December 28, 1983, Houston, Texas
Masters champion 1940, '47 and '50

Jimmy Demaret had an impish sense of humour and once spread the story that Sam Snead, who did not trust the banks, hid his money in tomato cans buried in his garden. Someone believed the tale and Snead arrived home unexpectedly one night to find the would-be thief digging up his lawn. Bob Hope called Demaret the funniest amateur comedian in the world. He once said: 'Golf and sex are about the only things you can enjoy without being good at them.' Demaret was also a talented singer and occasionally performed at a friend's nightclub in Galveston when not on tour. He also appeared in an episode of *I Love Lucy* on television.

Jimmy Demaret

The son of a carpenter and painter, Demaret thought the dull clothes worn on tour 'made it look like a funeral parlour out there'. Single-handedly, he changed all that, wearing lavender, gold, pink, orange, red and aqua trousers, and yellow, emerald, maroon, plaid, checked, striped and polka-dot sport coats. 'If you're going to be in the limelight,' he said, 'you might as well dress like it.' If it was Bing Crosby who popularised the pro-am format, it was Jimmy Demaret who made it worth playing with a pro.

'Jimmy Demaret enlivened the tour with his colourful clothes, a bright smile, and a uniquely splendid playing style,' Al Barkow wrote in *The History of the PGA Tour*. 'He walked up to the ball with a kind of short, rhythmic dance step, the club twirling in his hands, took a very narrow open stance and hit a lot of left-to-right cut shots.'

But Demaret was not to be underestimated. He won 31 official titles and was the first person to win the Masters three times. His first title in 1940 included a back nine of 30 in the first round, a record that stood for over 50 years. When he won in 1950, playing the last six holes in two under while runner-up Jim Ferrier played them in five over, the top ten included a who's who of the game: Snead, Ben Hogan, Byron Nelson, Lloyd Mangrum, Cary Middlecoff, Lawson Little and Gene Sarazen. In his three Ryder Cups, Demaret won all six of his contests.

A Texan just a couple of years older than Nelson and Hogan, he was an unlikely friend of the dour Hogan. They often paired together in fourball competitions. 'He was the most underrated golfer in history,' said Hogan. 'This man played shots I hadn't dreamed of. I learned them. But it was Jimmy who showed them to me first. He was the best wind player I've ever seen in my life.' Hogan thought that if Demaret would just practise, he would win every tournament he entered.

Demaret and Jackie Burke together set up the famous Champions Golf Club in Houston. Burke told *Golf Digest*: 'He played by feel and instinct, and he had a lot of imagination and guts. There was never a guy who was more fun to be around, or a guy who enjoyed being who he was, more than Jimmy.'

CARY MIDDLECOFF

Born January 6, 1921, Halls, Tennessee;
died September 1, 1998, Memphis, Tennessee
US Open champion 1949 and '56; Masters champion 1955

D entistry's loss was golf's gain. Cary Middlecoff had followed his father and two uncles in training as a dentist, which was enough for his colleagues on tour to call him 'Doc'. A fine amateur player in Memphis, who had never had a proper lesson, Middlecoff won the North and South Open in 1945 while playing alongside the great professionals Ben Hogan and Gene Sarazen in the final round. Two years later, having given up the chance to play in the Walker Cup, Middlecoff turned professional. 'I know I would never be happy practising dentistry without knowing for sure if I were a good player or a great one,' he explained later, 'and dentistry is too confining ever to offer me that opportunity.'

Middlecoff gave himself two years to make the grade or fall back on the family trade. In 1949 this 'happy refugee from sub gingival curettage', as Herb Warren Wind described him, won the US Open at Medinah. He went on to prove he was a great player, rather than just a good one, by winning the 1955 Masters by a then-record seven strokes, and a second US Open in 1956 by holding off Hogan and Julius Boros. From the mid-1940s to the end of the 1950s, only Hogan and Sam Snead won more titles on the PGA Tour.

A tall man who could hit the ball vast distances, he sometimes struggled with the short game and his temper. Once at a US Open at Oakmont he got so mad at himself, and a late starting time, that he smashed a ball onto the Pennsylvania Turnpike, which bisects the course, and stormed back to the clubhouse. He was also a very slow player, picking up Tommy Armour's mantle. In the playoff for the 1957 US Open, which Middlecoff had reached with a pair of 68s the previous day, his opponent Dick Mayer used a camping stool while Middlecoff played. Mayer won by seven shots.

For someone to whom the game seemed to come easily, and who proved himself under the highest pressure, there was hesitancy over

CARY MIDDLECOFF

which club to hit, as well as a super slow backswing which ground to a halt at the top. Robert Sommers wrote: 'Middlecoff was a mass of nerves. He was at once the fastest walker and slowest player on the tour. He moved along with quick, impatient strides, but once he reached the ball, he studied the shot for long and aggravating periods. He'd pick one club, then go back and pick another. He'd address the ball, then step away. Once over the ball, he'd set the club, then peek down the fairway, set the club, peek again. Endlessly. He chain-smoked. He fidgeted restlessly. He drove the gallery and the other players mad.' His colleagues joked that he gave up being a dentist because no one could keep their mouth open long enough.

A back injury ended his career in the early 1960 but he took to television commentary and wrote a highly acclaimed instruction book, *The Golf Swing*. He said: 'Nobody wins the Open. It wins you.' And: 'Anyone who hasn't been nervous, or hasn't choked somewhere down the line, is an idiot.'

JESSIE VALENTINE

Born March 18, 1915, Perth, Perthshire;
died April 6, 2006, Bridge of Earn, Perthshire
British Ladies Amateur champion 1937, '55 and '58

'Wee Jessie' was how she was known, but there was nothing small about her golfing achievements. Jessie Valentine dominated women's amateur golf for more than two decades in a career interrupted by the Second World War. She won the British Ladies three times and the Scottish Ladies six times, a record only beaten when Belle Robertson reached seven. She played with both Joyce Wethered and Babe Zaharias, and many Ryder Cup stalwarts such as Dai Rees and Eric Brown. In 1959 Jessie became the first woman to be honoured for her services to golf when she was awarded an MBE.

Jessie was the daughter of Joe Anderson, the first professional at Craigie Hill in Perth. Naturally, she grew up playing

JESSIE VALENTINE

at the club. Her first success came in 1933 at the British Girls Championship, though her father's reaction was: 'Is that all?' She won the national titles in New Zealand and France and made the first of her seven Curtis Cup appearances at Gleneagles in 1936, holing a long putt to tie the overall match. She won her first British Championship in 1937 and took the Scottish version in each of the next two years.

In the 1950s, her success continued. Twice more she won the British title, while she also lost in the final on two occasions, in 1950 to the Vicomtesse de St. Sauveur (nee Lally Vagliano), one of France's greatest players, and in 1957 to Philomena Garvey, of Ireland. Four more Scottish titles followed and in 1955 she became the first Scottish golfer to win the British and Scottish titles in the same year.

In the *Shell Encyclopedia of Golf*, Valentine is described thus: 'Like the majority of outstanding women players, she has always been good with all her woods. The control of her strokes with the irons is where she has always excelled, and in this department of the game, particularly on seaside courses, with unequal lies and stances, she has a mastery few women have equalled.'

At the age of 45 she relinquished her amateur status and took over her father's sports business and designed golf equipment for women. In 2002 she became an inaugural member of the Scottish Sport Hall of Fame. Shortly before her death at the age of 91 in 2006, the Craigie Hill website said: 'Jessie Valentine has brought the good name of Craigie Hill to the eyes of the world's golfing public more than any other name connected with the club. Jessie's achievements are only exceeded by her modesty and approachable friendliness and the club is enhanced by her honorary life membership.'

PATTY BERG

Born February 13, 1918, Minneapolis, Minnesota;
died September 10, 2006, Fort Myers, Florida
Titleholders champion 1937, '38, '39, '48, '53, '55 and '57;
US Women's Amateur champion 1938;
Western Open champion 1941, '43, '48, '51, '55, '57 and '58;
US Women's Open champion 1946

Patty Berg was a pioneer in the area of women's professional golf. She reckoned she gave over 16,000 clinics, which inspired countless thousands to take up the game. She was also the driving force behind the Ladies Professional Golf Association offering women professionals a similar circuit of tournaments as the PGA Tour did for the men. Plus, on the course, she still holds the record of 15 major titles and won over 80 tournaments as an amateur and professional.

Golf only came into her life after quarterbacking the neighbourhood football team, winning on the athletics track and becoming a speed skating champion. But her family were members of Interlachen and her father, Herman Berg, was her first coach. As a 17-year-old she lost to Glenna Collett Vare in the final of the US Amateur at her home course and was a runner-up again in 1937 before winning the next year. Her 28 amateur titles include three Titleholders Championships won as an amateur. One of the first big events for professionals, Berg won the Titleholders four more times among 57 victories as a professional. She also won the Western Open, another of what the LPGA has designated a 'major' of the era, seven times behind 1941 and '58, and won the inaugural US Women's Open in 1946.

She turned professional in 1940, the year after the death of her mother. Her father had subsidised her amateur career but she could start repaying him once she had signed with the Wilson sporting goods company to hold clinics all over the country. She was a natural showwoman – five foot, two inches, curly red hair, freckles, blue eyes and a smile always in place. 'I loved doing clinics and exhibitions,' she said. 'I did three a day but I could have done them all day and all night.'

Like the Wethered siblings before her, she charted every score and shot she played. That drive to succeed must have helped when

Patty Berg

her knee was broken in a car accident in 1941. She was in bed for five months and it took 18 months of operations and rehabilitation before she could play again, a comeback immediately rewarded with her second Western Open in 1943.

In 1950, Berg was the first president of the LPGA, having persuaded Wilson and promoter Fred Corcoran to back the venture. Berg was one of the stars, winning the money list three times but another was Babe Zaharias. Babe took all the headlines but Mickey Wright said: 'Babe couldn't carry Patty Berg's golf clubs. She is the consummate perfect golfer for a woman, which shows in the fact she could still swing the club as beautifully, and with all the class, in her sixties as earlier in her career.'

In 1951, Berg led a team of American women professionals, including Zaharias, to take on British male amateurs at Wentworth. Trailing 2½-½ after the foursomes, their lunch table was quiet until Berg got up and announced: 'All those who expect to win their singles, follow me.' Zaharias added: 'C'mon, follow Napoleon.' They swept the six singles to win 6½-2½.

BABE ZAHARIAS

Born June 26, 1911, Port Arthur, Texas;
died, September 27, 1956, Forth Worth, Texas
Western Open champion 1940, '44, '45 and '50;
US Women's Amateur champion 1946; British Ladies Amateur
champion 1947; Titleholders champion 1947, '50 and '52;
US Women's Open 1948, '50 and '54

Asked if there was anything she didn't play, Babe Zaharias replied: 'Yes. Dolls.' Mildred Didrikson, as she was then named, played, or rather excelled at, basketball, tennis, swimming, diving, bowling and baseball – she hit so many home runs she was nicknamed 'Babe' after baseball star Babe Ruth and the name stuck forever. At the trials for the 1932 Olympics she entered eight events, won six and set four world records. At the Los Angeles

Babe Zaharias

Games themselves she was restricted to three events and won gold medals in the javelin and the 80m hurdles, while she matched the winner's new world record in the high jump but was demoted to the silver because her futuristic Western Roll technique was not yet legal. Grantland Rice, a senior sports writer of the day, wrote she was the 'Ultimate Amazon and the greatest athlete of all mankind for all time.'

Then came golf. 'I took a fling at many other sports but when the golf bug hit me it was fatal,' she said. She won her first amateur event in 1935 but was barred for being a professional in other sports. The sixth of seven children of Norwegian immigrants, she was from a poor part of Texas and needed to earn a living so took her place on the exhibition circuit.

She was to change the women's game. 'Until Babe came along,' said Patty Berg, 'women were all swing and no hit. She put power into women's golf.' An athlete and a supreme competitor, Babe also knew she had to learn how to play the game – she had out-hit Joyce Wethered in their 1935 exhibitions but been comfortably outscored. 'My formula for success was simple: practice and concentration. I was determined to play the game well, or not at all.'

After marrying wrestler George Zaharias, the 'Crying Greek from Cripple Creek', Babe went through the lengthy process of restoring her amateur status. During a run of 27 wins from 28 events, she won the US Amateur in 1946, never going beyond the 15th hole, and the British Ladies the following year at Gullane, where she lost only four holes. Enid Wilson wrote that she 'moves like a ballerina, as though she does not have a bone in her body. She is so fit that sheer joie de vivre prevents her from being motionless. Unless I had been at Gullane, I would not have believed it humanly possible for a woman to hit a golf ball as far as she did.'

Babe turned professional again and was the star of the new LPGA circuit, winning one in four of the events she played. Her greatest triumphs were the three US Open titles but the greatest of all was the one in 1954 when she won by 12 strokes a year after overcoming cancer. The disease returned and she died two years later at the age of 45. 'Honey, I ain't going to die,' were her last words to her husband.

President Eisenhower opened his remarks that day talking about Babe. Patty Berg said, 'She was a great friend and the greatest woman athlete I ever saw. She died before she could see the result of all the doors she opened. It was very sad, a tremendous loss.'

LOUISE SUGGS

Born September 7, 1923, Atlanta, Georgia
Western Open champion 1946, '47, '49 and '53;
Titleholders champion 1946, '54, '56 and '59; US Women's
Amateur champion 1947; British Ladies Amateur champion 1948;
US Women's Open 1949 and '52; LPGA champion 1957

Louise Suggs was the third star of the women's game in America along with Patty Berg and Babe Zaharias when the LPGA was born. Inevitably, they were the main contenders, so much so that Suggs said it was like watching 'three cats fighting over a plate of fish'. She was a far more reserved character than Berg or Babe, whom Suggs seemed particularly to resent for the way her knack for publicity overshadowed everyone else. At least on one occasion Suggs had the satisfaction of beating Zaharias into second place in the 1949 US Women's Open by a massive 14 strokes, still a record for the championship.

Suggs was the daughter of John Suggs, a pitcher for the New York Yankees who settled in Atlanta and became the manager of a golf course in Lithia Springs, Georgia. Her dad showed her the fundamentals of grip and stance and then told her to 'keep slamming the ball'. So she did and was later nicknamed 'Miss Sluggs' by Bob Hope. She played often with Bobby Jones and in 2007 was awarded the USGA's highest honour, the Bob Jones award. She said: 'Being a native Atlantan I admired and respected him immensely, and I even patterned my own game after him. To be honoured with this award is the ultimate accolade I could possibly receive.'

Suggs also played with Ben Hogan, who said: 'We won a pro-lady event and seeing her fine shot-making, to me her later

LOUISE SUGGS

victories were the logical result. Her swing was a beautiful thing – so smooth and rhythmic, so soundly joined together – she was bound to be a winner.'

Her amateur career included a Titleholders and two Western Opens, both of which she would win again as a professional, and the 1947 US Women's Amateur and the 1948 British Ladies title. She was the second American to win the British, a year after Zaharias, then she turned professional and became one of the 13 founder members of the LPGA. She won 55 times as a pro and her 11 major wins place her third on the LPGA's list behind only Berg and Mickey Wright. She won a second US Women's Open in 1952 and the LPGA Championship in its third year in 1957.

Her winning run ended in 1962, the last year she played the tour full-time, following a dispute with the LPGA about a standard fine of $25 imposed for entering a tournament and not turning up. She was later reconciled with the organisation she helped so much in the early days and she has raised the American flag at recent Solheim Cups. For over 50 years she was based at Sea Island, and among her grateful clients there were the future President George HW Bush and his wife Barbara.

'Louise was a very talented golfer, without question one of the best players we ever had,' said Betsy Rawls. 'She had one of the best swings, was one of the best putters and a great competitor. I always liked her and enjoyed her. She is an interesting person, very intelligent, and if she feels comfortable and appreciated, she is fun to be around.'

BETSY RAWLS

Born May 4, 1928, Spartanburg, South Carolina
US Women's Open champion 1951, '53, '57 and '60; Western Open champion 1952 and '59; LPGA champion 1959 and '69

It was a leap of faith for a woman to turn professional in the post-War era, but Betsy Rawls must have been unique in doing so after collecting a degree in physics at the University of Texas. There is a

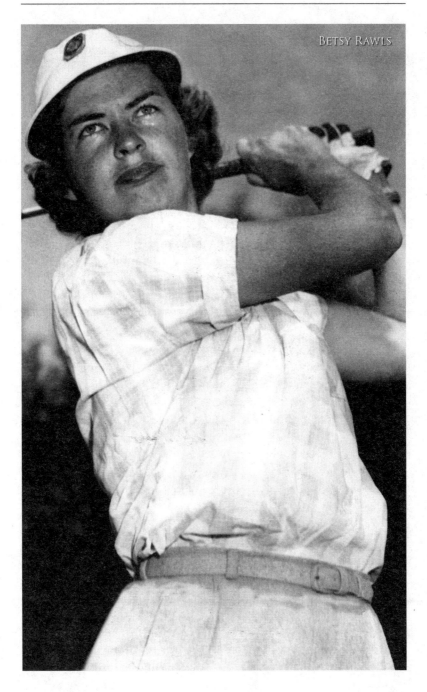

BETSY RAWLS

marvellous photograph in Liz Kahn's history of the LPGA which shows Rawls, arm resting on a suitcase, reading Bertrand Russell's *A History of Western Philosophy*. A little light reading, indeed.

'Although I always read a lot and was interested in other things, all I wanted to do was play golf, think about it and practise,' Rawls said. 'It's not necessarily a good thing to be so totally absorbed because it's very narrow and limited, but winning makes it all worth it. Nothing can make you feel quite as good as winning a golf tournament.'

Rawls assured her place in history by winning the US Women's Open four times. Only Mickey Wright has matched that feat. She also won two LPGA Championship and the Western Open twice, among 55 professional victories. In 1950 she was runner-up at the US Open as an amateur and then she turned professional and, as well as becoming one of Patty Berg's apprentices on the exhibition circuit, won the national championship in her rookie season. 'Winning my first US Open didn't seem so important at the time,' she said. 'I thought if I didn't win that one, I could always win the next. My biggest thrill was the LPGA in 1969 because by then I wasn't sure I could win again.'

She had taken up golf at the age of 17 and when she got interested she went to see Harvey Penick, the legendary coach and the head pro at Austin Country Club. Penick charged her $1.50 for the first lesson and then never charged her again – he never did accept payment from his star pupils. He remained Rawls's only coach. 'Harvey reduced golf, as he did life, to a few sound, irrefutable, worthwhile principles,' she said. 'He was always a refuge from the complexities and emotional traumas of the tour. To come back and see Harvey was to become refreshed, to become inspired and to be able to put things in perspective once more.'

Rawls mucked in, doing all the jobs the players did to get the LPGA going, acting as secretary, president and tournament committee chair. 'The players made the pairings, kept statistics, set up the course, did a lot of hard work. Sport is selfish, but off the course you completely changed your way of thinking so that it was for the good of the organisation. The players today don't know how easy they have it.'

After her playing career, Rawls became a tournament director for the LPGA, then ran the LPGA Championship. In 1980 she became the first woman to serve on the rules committee at the men's US Open. Kahn, who got to know Rawls well in her later life, wrote: 'She is a shy woman for whom I feel much warmth and affection. I enjoy her mind and her company.'

INTERNATIONAL EXPANSION 1950–1960

B obby Locke was the first great champion to come from outside Britain or America. He was the first of many fine South African players such as Gary Player, Ernie Els and Retief Goosen. He was a superb putter who rolled them in from all over the green. With Locke, the game began to expand its horizons around the globe. Norman Von Nida was a pioneer in Australia, followed by Peter Thomson, who brought a considered, intellectual approach to links golf and who emulated Taylor and Braid's five Open victories. Flory Van Donck led the way in Europe, while Christy O'Connor Snr showed that an Irishman could match Sam Snead for a swing with grace and elegance. Amateurs were still big news and Joe Carr was Ireland's most famous player, while Sir Michael Bonallack began a career which saw him dominate the scene in Britain in a prelude to a long and successful administrative career with the R&A. In Canada, Marlene Stewart Streit was peerless, reducing many an opponent to a crumpled mess thanks to her relentless putting. Her compatriot, Moe Norman, had an unorthodox swing but was the straightest hitter of all time and, despite withdrawing early from competing at the highest level, was still a genius who was only really appreciated late in life.

BOBBY LOCKE

Born November 20, 1917, Germiston, South Africa;
died March 9, 1987, Johannesburg, South Africa
Open champion 1949, '50, '52 and '57

Until now, Arnaud Massy aside, the game had been dominated by Britain and America. This was about to change. Jim
Ferrier was an Australian who had emigrated to America before
he won the 1947 USPGA but the game's expansion became obvious when Bobby Locke and Peter Thomson won eight out of ten
Opens between 1949 and '58, with Gary Player and Kel Nagle
winning the next two. The only interlopers were Max Faulkner,
who prevented Locke's hat-trick of titles in 1951, and Ben Hogan
in 1953.

He was christened Arthur D'Arcy Locke, but his father named
him after his hero, Bobby Jones. Where Locke surpassed even
Jones was in being one of the game's greatest ever putters. 'Very
early in my career I realised that putting was half the game of
golf,' he said. 'No matter how well I might play the long shots,
if I couldn't putt I would never win.' Just as he played with a
pronounced hook with the long clubs, Locke developed a closed-
stance putting style, which pulled the ball from right-to-left and
was effective on any surface.

He used the same hickory-shafted putter which had been given
to him when he was nine. Peter Alliss once hit some putts with it.
'The moment it was in your hands you had the same feeling a violinist must get when allowed to hold a Stradivarius,' Alliss said.
'When you put the club behind the ball you felt it wanted to swing
the way the master swung it – eerie.' Sam Snead said: 'He'd hit a
50-footer and before the ball got halfway he'd be tipping his hat to
the crowd.' Snead might have beaten Locke into second place at the
1946 Open but in a series of exhibitions in South Africa between the
two, Locke won 12 of the 16 matches.

On the strength of that performance, Locke went to America and
in two-and-a-half years won 11 of 59 events with ten second places.
Once he won by 16 strokes. The locals were not happy. They called

BOBBY
LOCKE

the jowly Locke 'Old Muffin Face' or 'Old Baggy Pants', since he often wore plus-fours. One promoter who did not want Locke to win his event was told by other players to put the pins on the right of every green, since Locke hooked the ball. The tactic worked but ignored the fact that he was a great chipper of the ball. In 1949, having missed a couple of tournaments he had entered, Locke was banned by the Tour. Gene Sarazen called it the 'most disgraceful action by any golf organisation'. Although the ban was soon lifted, Locke was ever after happier playing in Britain.

In 1960, Locke almost died and he lost the sight in his left eye after his car was hit by a train at a level crossing. He played only rarely after that and died of meningitis in 1987, while his surviving wife and daughter, who had become increasingly eccentric, tragically committed suicide together some years later.

FLORY VAN DONCK

Born June 23, 1912, Tervuren, Belgium;
died January 14, 1992 (location unconfirmed)

Flory Van Donck never won the Open but the *Sunday Chronicle Cricket and Golf Annuals* of the early 1950s list him as one of the 'Stars to follow' and described him as a 'frequent and popular visitor from Belgium.' The son of a greenkeeper from Brussels, Van Donck became the finest player on the continent of Europe between Arnaud Massy and the Ballesteros-Langer era. He won in Britain but was prolific in Europe, winning seven times in 1953 to claim the Vardon Trophy as winner of the order of merit.

The national Opens on the European continent had been running for some time. The French Open dates from 1906, the Belgian Open from 1910, the German Open from 1911, the Dutch Open from 1912, the Swiss Open from 1923 and the Italian Open from 1925. Of these, the French was the most important, having been won four times by Massy, twice by JH Taylor and Henry Cotton and once each by James Braid and Walter Hagen. Bobby Locke

FLORY VAN
DONCK

won it in 1952 and '53, and Byron Nelson, with a superb display of iron shots despite having retired from full-time golf a decade earlier, in 1955. Van Donck won the French Open three times, in 1954, '57 and '58.

Pat Ward-Thomas, in *Not Only Golf*, described the scene at the French Open of that time: 'Invariably the championship came after the Open in Britain and made a soothing contrast. Flory Van Donck, with his courtly manner and perfect style, and Robert de Vicenzo often played supremely well in France, and watching was a pleasure because there were only a hundred or so spectators. Quite often they included the Duke of Windsor who made a most agreeable and keen watching companion. He was always interested in the Argentinean players, Vicenzo, Tony Cerda and others and would hasten in pursuit of them.'

Van Donck dominated golf in his home country, winning the Belgium Professional title 16 times between 1939–56. He also won the Belgium Open five times, the Dutch five times, the Italian four times, the German and Swiss Opens twice and the Portuguese Open once. He represented his country many times in the Canada Cup, which became the World Cup, including as a 67-year-old in 1979. In 1960 he took the individual honours ahead of the likes of Snead, Palmer, Locke, Player and Nagle.

In the Open Van Donck finished in the top ten in all but two years between 1948 and 1959, and was also twice runner-up, in 1956 to Peter Thomson and in 1959 to Gary Player. In 1956 at Hoylake, when the rules allowed a player to leave the flagstick in the hole even while putting, he saw putts hit the pin twice and bounce out both times.

Tall with an unorthodox swing, Van Donck was a fine putter, despite holding the shaft with his hands separated and low and with the toe of the putter cocked in the air, as Isao Aoki did later on. 'A prince among golfers,' pronounced Donald Steel.

NORMAN
VON NIDA

NORMAN VON NIDA

Born February 14, 1914, Strathfield, Australia;
died May 20, 2007, Gold Coast, Australia

Norman Von Nida was never the biggest man but he had quali-ties for golf that were honed in the most unorthodox fashion – between rounds caddying at Royal Queensland he was working at an abattoir. 'I had to break open the heads of sheep after their skulls had been partially split by a machine. My forearms, hands and fingers became incredibly strong ... and I was unbeatable in an arm wrestle against anyone my size.'

Von Nida is the 'father' of Australian golf. He was the first Australian to travel around the world, winning the Philippine Open in 1938 and '39 after a three-week boat journey there and back each time, and then becoming a leading player in Europe after the Second World War. He was a contrast in many ways. He was a tough com-petitor. He arrived in Britain in 1946 with £17 in his pocket and had to win to make money. He won twice that year and seven times the next year, claiming the Vardon Trophy.

He had a temper. He never played much in America after one incident in 1948 when he and his playing partner got into a score-card dispute after a round and had to be separated by the police as they traded blows in front of the clubhouse.

Dennis Von Nida, his estranged son by his first marriage, claimed after his father's death that he never shared his winnings with his fam-ily but among Australia's golfers he was known as a generous mentor, whether with his time or even lending money to a player so he could stay on tour. Peter Thomson, David Graham, Bruce Crampton and Jack Newton were thankful for Von Nida's help in their careers.

In the Open, between 1946 and '48, Von Nida was fourth, sixth and third. The joint third-round leader in 1947, he fell back with a 76. He called his three Australian Open titles his biggest achievement but he was also the runner-up six times. In discussing the distrac-tions that afflict golfers, such as the 'roar of butterflies in an adjacent meadow,' as PG Wodehouse put it, Henry Longhurst wrote: 'From reading his book I fancy that Von Nida would have won a post-war championship if part of his mind had not been engaged on looking for things or people which could later be held to have put him off.'

Late in his life Von Nida went blind but still played golf. 'All I've got to do is swing the club and allow someone to tell me where it went,' he said. 'I can tell by the feel of the club contacting the ball, relatively in what direction it's gone and how far it's gone.' He also continued to offer lessons by listening to the sound of contact between club and ball. In 1998 at Royal Adelaide he advised Nick Faldo, after an opening 77, that his left-hand grip was too tight. Faldo said his golf was 'like a new day' when he scored a 69 in the second round.

PETER THOMSON

Born August 23, 1929, Melbourne, Australia
Open champion 1954, '55, '56, '58 and '65

Can a golfer be too intelligent to be a great champion? Peter Thomson is the first witness for the defence, personification in golf of CLR James's famous aphorism: 'What does he know of cricket who only cricket knows?' Pat Ward-Thomas visited Thomson in Melbourne: 'In his home one would be pressed to find any evidence that he had played the game seriously. I saw no cases of trophies, no array of medals and, as I recall, few golf books in his library. Thomson is a man of varied tastes as could be judged by the people one met in his house. Although playing golf, designing courses and writing have been his profession he and his appealing wife Mary, do not seem to allow them to obtrude into their private life.'

Among Thomson's few failures was a narrow defeat when he stood for the Australian parliament, although his son Andrew did succeed in politics and became the minister for sport and tourism. Another relative failure was his record in America, where he won just once. But on the Seniors tour, that great career mulligan, he won nine times in 1985 at the age of 56. He promptly went back to writing (never with a ghostwriter), commentating and designing courses. Late in life he liked nothing better than spending the summer months

Peter Thomson

in St. Andrews, while in his pioneering days of travelling around Asia and Europe, he often went sightseeing instead of practising.

Thomson thought the game a simple matter. With the proper fundamentals of grip, alignment and posture, the swing followed naturally. If he ever needed to correct a fault, he would head for an armchair, think it through, and go out to hit balls to confirm his diagnosis. Growing up in Melbourne, he relished hard and fast courses and the links of Britain were perfect for him. He often eschewed a driver but hit long-iron shots low with plenty of roll, while he mastered the art of running up an approach to the green. 'Thomson was the first person to play golf as if it were chess,' said Peter Alliss. John Jacobs said: 'He plotted his way around a course, always keeping the ball in play.' 'Peter is the only player I have ever been on a course with whose swing got slower as the situation got tighter,' said George Will, the Scottish Ryder Cup golfer.

At the Open Thomson was exceptional. From his debut in 1951 to '71 he was only out of the top-nine three times. In seven Opens from 1952 his finishes were: second (to Locke), second (to Hogan), first, first, first, second (to Locke), first. He was the only player in the 20th century to win a hat-trick of titles, and if the strength of the fields in the 1950s was not quite as strong as it would become in subsequent decades, he won a fifth title in 1965 against American stars such as Palmer, Nicklaus and Lema. He joined James Braid and JH Taylor with five wins, only matched since by Tom Watson, and only surpassed by Harry Vardon.

KEL NAGLE

Born December 21, 1920, North Sydney, Australia
Open champion 1960

When the 150th anniversary Open Championship took place at St. Andrews in 2010, one absent friend was the winner of the Centenary Open, Kel Nagle, the oldest surviving Open champion. Travelling for the 89-year-old was out of the question but he

Kel
Nagle

was busy at home sharing memories with his four children, eight grandchildren and six great-grandchildren. It was a surprise victory in 1960, also at St. Andrews, as the 39-year-old Australian held off Arnold Palmer in his full pomp. The winner of that year's Masters and US Open, Palmer was charging hard and birdied the 18th while Nagle watched from the 17th green. As well as seeing Palmer hole out, the mighty roar that went up told Nagle he needed to hole his eight-footer for par to stay one stroke ahead. He did. It was one of the great pressure putts in championship golf. At the last, his four-footer for a birdie lipped out to a foot. Nagle recalled: 'I could hear Henry Longhurst in the commentary box saying, "Be careful, be careful." It went in pretty hard.'

Palmer had failed to match Ben Hogan's three major titles in one year but, arguably, it was the best result for the Open. Palmer came back the next year to win the claret jug, and did so again in 1962, when Nagle was the runner-up. Palmer kept coming back and brought all the other great Americans with him.

The one person who thought Nagle would win was Peter Thomson. The pair were firm friends and it was the younger man who encouraged Nagle to once again try his luck in Britain after two undistinguished appearances early in the 1950s. A wild player in his younger days, Nagle gradually learnt how to play more steadily, keeping the ball in play, his development no doubt helped by playing with Thomson. The pair won the Canada Cup for Australia in 1954 and '59, the latter on home soil at Royal Melbourne. It was then that Thomson told Nagle: 'You're playing well. You're driving well, your irons are good and you're putting good. You can win the Open.' When they arrived at St. Andrews, Thomson showed Nagle the tricks of the Old Course. He learnt well.

Nagle was a contender at the Open throughout the 1960s and lost a playoff for the US Open to Gary Player in 1965. Thomson said: 'There was absolutely no malice in him, or vice of any kind, and he was always in good humour.'

Player added: 'I can honestly say I never met anybody in my life that didn't really like Kel Nagle.' Yet the late Henry Cooper said this of playing in a pro-am for the first time alongside Nagle: 'I was sweating up. I could feel my legs trembling like I'd been hit by a perfect left hook and the palms of my hands were moist. I don't think I ever felt more nervous than I did that day before any of my fights, whether they were championship fights or stepping into the ring with Ali.'

CHRISTY O'CONNOR SNR

Born December 21, 1924, Galway, Ireland

Irishman Fred Daly won the Open in 1947 and his 'round, loveable' compatriot Harry Bradshaw might have done so a year later but for the incident of playing out of a broken bottle rather than asking for relief. Christy O'Connor, however, was probably the greatest Irish golfer of his era. Peter Dobereiner summed up how he should be remembered. 'Christy is a difficult man to place in the pecking order of the golfing greats because his record lacks a single major championship. But you only have to see his fluid, self-taught swing to appreciate that this is no first-class second-rater but a man to be numbered among the very best in the history of golf.'

Henry Longhurst wrote he swung the club 'by the pure light of nature'. Lee Trevino said: 'To me, only three players have ever looked entirely natural swinging a golf club – Christy O'Connor, Roberto de Vicenzo and Neil Coles. Christy flows through the ball like fine wine.' Coles, incidentally, along with O'Connor, dominated the British professional scene for years, winning in six different decades. The longevity of O'Connor's swing was demonstrated by his six wins in eight years at the PGA Seniors Championship.

The son of a farmer, his swing was honed in Galway and could be adapted to all weathers and clubs. The legendary story goes, details varying in the telling, of a young pup boasting about hitting a shorter club into a par-three than Himself, as O'Connor was known, who promptly found the green with every club in his bag, including the putter. Then there was a centenary exhibition at Westward Ho! in 1964 where O'Connor and Max Faulkner played in Norfolk jackets, breeches and deerstalkers with five hickory clubs against the

CHRISTY O'CONNOR SNR

modern attire and equipment of Peter Alliss and Brian Huggett. The 'ancients' received shots but O'Connor, the star throughout, fading, drawing, hitting low or high at will, sealed the win by pitching in from 35 yards over a stream at the last hole.

'Himself was a genius, a legend,' said Alliss, who was his four-somes partner for many of O'Connor's ten successive Ryder Cups. O'Connor and Bradshaw won the Canada Cup for Ireland in 1958 in Mexico City but at the Open he had three near-misses out of 11 top-tens. He won 24 times in Britain and Ireland, including the first ever four-figure and five-figure winner's cheques. His putting was not up to the rest of his game but Pat Ward-Thomas called him an 'amiable soul who enjoyed the convivial things in life and was the most accom-plished stroke-maker of the post-Cotton generation in these isles.'

Once, after a fog delay had ruled out play the previous day, O'Connor was feeling the worse for wear the next morning, so he ordered a golf writer to collect a jug of black coffee, containing the hair of the dog, and to proceed 250 yards down the right side of the first fairway and head 20 yards into the woods. A ball arrived at the precise spot, followed by Himself, who drained the lot.

JOE CARR

Born February 22, 1922, Dublin, Ireland;
died June 3, 2004, Dublin, Ireland
Amateur champion 1953, '58 and '60

In the 1959 Dunlop Masters at Portmarnock, Christy O'Connor saved the blushes of the professionals by coming from four strokes behind in the last round to beat Joe Carr. A year later, Carr was two off the lead of Kel Nagle at the Centenary Open when he made a cracking start to the final round, only for a storm to wash out the day. The scores did not count, the round started afresh the next day and Carr dropped to eighth place.

Carr was an amateur but that was no bar to him being possibly the biggest personality in the game in Britain and Ireland after the

JOE CARR

War. 'He became the most popular citizen in all of Ireland,' wrote Pat Ward-Thomas, 'not only because of his golf but because of an appealingly uninhibited outlook, gentleness of spirit and charming manners to everyone with whom he was in contact. In victory he was always modest and chivalrous towards opponents; while defeat was accepted with good humour and grace.'

He was lean and lanky, a dashing golfer who hit the ball huge distances and often came up with wonderful recoveries. He was bold, a great exponent of head-to-head matchplay, a ruthless winner but also a good loser. As a baby he was adopted by his mother's sister, who was the stewardess, and her husband the steward, at Portmarnock. Later in life, he would hit balls in the morning from his back garden onto neighbouring Sutton Golf Club and then head into Dublin to work in his clothing business. He won the British Amateur three times, played in 11 Walker Cups, and was captain when Britain and Ireland tied in Baltimore in 1965, a rare non-defeat.

Carr was naturally a team man and his contribution was as much off the course as on it, for his record appears better as an individual than on international duty, when he would wear a white cap with a green pom-pom. Henry Longhurst observed: 'In team matches he has carried an appallingly heavy load of responsibility. He has always been our trump card, the one card that is expected surely to win us a trick, and I believe this has borne heavily on him.' Carr was constantly urged by spectators to 'Have a go, Joe!' and according to Longhurst he did just that. 'It still gives me a pleasure to see Joe lash out at one. There are those, though not many, who hit it as far, but none in my opinion who hit it with such controlled abandon.'

Carr was the first non-American to be awarded the Bob Jones award for sportsmanship by the USGA in 1967 and was the first Irishman to become captain of the R&A in 1991, apparently going for a dip in St. Andrews Bay prior to the driving-in ceremony to sober up after a fine party the night before. 'I consider myself very fortunate to have played golf in the Joe Carr era,' said Michael Bonallack. 'I still have yet to meet a finer sportsman.'

Sir Michael Bonallack

Born December 31, 1934, Chigwell, Essex
Amateur champion 1961, '65, '68, '69 and '70

In 1968, Michael Bonallack beat Joe Carr in the final of the Amateur Championship at Troon. Bonallack beat everyone that year. It was also the start of a hat-trick of Amateur wins, a unique feat. His tally of five Amateurs remains second only to John Ball's eight but his five English Amateur titles and his four English Strokeplay titles are records. He won all three in 1968. He was not quite the last of the career amateurs. Peter McEvoy, now an innovator as the brains behind PowerPlay Golf, the new nine-hole format with two pins per green, won two Amateurs, as did Gary Wolstenholme, who turned professional to join the Seniors tour. These days, youngsters barely stay amateur long enough to play in multiple Amateurs, let alone win them. Bonallack never thought he was good enough, at least not until later in his career when the titles kept stacking up.

People underestimated Bonallack. At one Amateur, Scotland's Gordon Cosh asked: 'Who is that? And how does he get a handicap low enough to play in this?' The answer was Bonallack and he was the defending champion. His swing was likened to 'heaving a sack of coal into the cellar', while when putting he spread his legs wide, crouching low as if sniffing the top of the putter handle. But his was a triumph of substance over style. When it mattered, the putts went in. In one championship final, he got up-and-down from off the green 22 times, more than enough to crush the spirit of his opponent. He had the champion's ability to raise his game or make a decisive thrust, always with a friendly countenance but also ruthless determination. 'Year after year writing of his golf became an exercise in restraint of superlatives and seeking varied phrases with which to analyse and praise him,' said golf writer Pat Ward-Thomas.

Both his sister Sally and wife Angela were golfing champions and played in the Curtis Cup, as Bonallack did nine times in the Walker Cup. His crowning glory was as playing captain when Britain and

Sir Michael
Bonallack

Ireland beat America for only the second time at St. Andrews in 1971. 'It does not get, it cannot get, any better than that,' he said. Ward-Thomas wrote: 'The triumph belonged first and foremost to Bonallack who, in his calm, unshakeable fashion, had instilled in his team confidence and faith in their ability to win. He said later that he had never doubted their capacity to do so. That they succeeded was his fitting reward.'

Bonallack later filled many administrative roles but when asked to consider becoming secretary of the R&A replied: 'Don't be bloody stupid.' He reconsidered and was praised for his stewardship of the game and the Open between 1983 and 1999. He is one of four golfing knights along with Henry Cotton, Bob Charles and Nick Faldo. Telling his wife she would no longer be 'Mrs Bonallack', Angela gasped: 'Who is she and do I know her?' before he could say that from now on she would be 'Lady Bonallack'.

MARLENE STEWART STREIT

Born March 9, 1934, Cereal, Alberta, Canada
British Ladies Amateur champion 1953;
US Women's Amateur champion 1956

Another lifelong amateur champion was Marlene Streit (*née* Stewart). And by 'lifelong', consider the fact that she won her first Canadian Amateur as a 17-year-old and her third US Women's Senior Amateur as a 69-year-old. A few days after her 77th birthday in 2011 she scored a 73. Although ranked third behind Mike Weir, the 2003 Masters champion, and George Knudson in *SCOREGolf* magazine's list of the top-25 best Canadian golfers, many still consider Streit the greatest. She is the only Canadian inducted into the World Golf Hall of Fame.

Her record is amazing. She won the Canadian Amateur 11 times in 22 years. She faced the same opponent, Miss M Gay, in three of those finals and won 9 and 8, 11 and 9, and 8 and 6. She won her national closed championship nine times, including seven times

MARLENE STEWART STREIT

Moe Norman

in a row in the 1950s. She won the British Amateur in 1953 and 10,000 people turned out to see her paraded in an open-topped car on her return to Toronto. She won the US Amateur in 1956 beating JoAnne Gunderson (later Carner) in the final. Ten years later Gunderson had her revenge but only at the 41st hole. Streit is the only golfer to have won the Amateur titles of Britain, America, Canada and Australia.

She started caddying at Lookout Point in Fonthill, Ontario at 13 and two years later started swinging a club. The club professional, Gordon McInnis, was the only coach she ever had. She never grew much over five foot tall but said the key to her swing was 'smoothness, rhythm and balance', and added: 'I was uncomplicated. I didn't have a million thoughts and I didn't have a million people telling me how to do it. I had one person telling me how to do it.'

Streit had a good short game and was a brilliant putter. She said she did not need to develop a winning instinct, it was just always there. They say you can only beat the people in front of you but, even though Streit never turned professional, she never cared about her opponent's reputation. 'I wasn't intimidated by anybody,' she said. 'It didn't matter if they were well-known Americans. I didn't like to lose to anyone.'

Streit played in the '*Shell's Wonderful World of Golf*' series and beat Marilynn Smith in Oslo but lost to Mickey Wright the following year. She earned $10,000 for her appearances but to protect her amateur status donated the money to what became the Marlene Streit Awards Fund. Young Canadian golfers are still being helped with travelling expenses from the fund. One such, Nancy Harvey, who went on to spend 15 years on the LPGA, said: 'There's a great deal of us that, who knows where we would've gotten if it weren't for Marlene. She believed in us and if Marlene believed in you, you were definitely going somewhere.'

MOE NORMAN

Born July 10, 1929, Kitchener, Ontario, Canada;
died September 4, 2004, Kitchener, Ontario, Canada

P eter Dobereiner said that Moe Norman was the greatest golfer 'who chose not to play championships'. Norman's record at the highest level cannot be compared to anyone else's because he does not have one. Whether that was because he chose not to, or simply could not compete under the greatest pressure, is almost irrelevant. Because Norman was a genius and a legend. Sam Snead and Lee Trevino said Norman was the greatest ball-striker they had ever seen. Tiger Woods said: 'Only two players have ever truly owned their swings – Moe Norman and Ben Hogan. I want to own mine. That's where the satisfaction comes from.'

Hogan called any shot that went dead straight an 'accident'. He watched Norman on the practice range once in the 1950s and muttered 'accident' after each of the first half-dozen shots. After a few more shots he walked away telling Norman: 'Just keep hitting those accidents.' His accuracy was bewildering to other players. In an exhibition match in Toronto in 1969, Snead laid up in front of a creek that crossed the fairway at 240 yards. Warned by Snead he could not make the carry, Norman merely said he was not trying to carry the water, he was aiming for the bridge. His drive duly landed short, rolled over the bridge and made it safely to the other side.

All the more amazing was that Norman achieved such accuracy from a swing that was purely of his own making and has not been replicated by any other player of standing. He stood straight-legged with feet wide apart and extended his arms as far as he could in front of him. The head of the club was a foot away from the ball rather than directly behind it. He had a short, quick backswing but then he did everything quickly, on the green barely steadying himself over the ball before striking the putt. Clearly, he could putt well at a certain level but on the bigger stages it was a weakness. Nor did he seem to have much desire to score well, or to win. He once walked in from the course after hitting the flagstick on the first three holes. 'Why go on? Can't do any better than that.'

Norman was only happy when hitting golf shots. He was shy, afraid of crowds and had an inferiority complex. He won the Canadian Amateur in 1955 and '56, all manner of provincial tournaments and countless professional events in Canada. But his spell on the USPGA Tour in the late 1950s was short-lived. A player reprimanded him for his clothing and the officials were not happy with his teeing up balls on Coke cans and six-inch tees during tournaments. Instead, he roamed Canada and Florida in the winter, living in motels and his car, playing exhibitions. He broke 33 course records. From 1995 until his death nine years later, Wally Uihlein, of equipment company Titleist, paid Norman $5,000 a month merely for 'being Moe Norman'.

THE BIG THREE
1960–1970

A rnold Palmer was the most thrilling golfer in America at the time that television started broadcasting the game. He revolutionised the perception of the sport with his exciting brand of golf. Whether they watched him on television or lined the fairways, Arnie's Army brought new fans to the game. But almost before the King had been crowned, so came along the Golden Bear. Jack Nicklaus won more of the biggest tournaments for longer than anyone else in the history of the game. From the US Open in 1962 to the Masters in 1986, he was golf's gold standard. And if there was to be a third member of golf's latest superstar trio, Gary Player was a worthy inclusion. The South African travelled more than anyone else and still managed to win nine major championships. The Big Three was how they were marketed by Mark McCormack, who founded the International Management Group, and he was not wrong. But, in contrast, truly out on her own was Mickey Wright who dominated the women's game in this era, and who might just have had the best swing of anyone, male or female.

TOMMY BOLT

Born March 31, 1916, Haworth, Oklahoma;
died August 30, 2008, Batesville, Arkansas
US Open champion 1958

Tommy Bolt had one of the sweetest swings in the business but that is not why people watched him. His mentor, Ben Hogan, once said: 'If I could only have screwed another head on Tommy's shoulders, he could have been the best player that ever played.'

He was called 'Terrible Tommy', 'Thunder Bolt' and 'the Vesuvius of golf' for the very good reason that his temper often got the better of him. This was the handicap he overcame to win the most frustrating championship of all, the US Open, in 1958 at Southern Hills in the intense summer heat of Oklahoma. That week he was all smiles, joking with the gallery and the press. Less than impressed with a newspaper report that said he was 49, Bolt claimed he was 39. 'It was just a typographical error,' he was told. 'Typographical error, my ass,' he replied. 'It was a perfect four and a perfect nine.' Bolt was actually 42, but that only came to light much later.

It was Bolt who advised, in the style of instruction articles for the swing, on how to throw a club. 'Always throw it forward,' he said. 'It takes less energy than having to walk back for your club.' Often he would not bother throwing a club, just put it over his knee and snap the shaft. 'It thrills crowds to see a guy suffer,' he said. 'That's why I threw clubs so often. They love to see golf get the better of someone.' Faced with a short approach shot at Pebble Beach once, his caddie offered him a choice between a three-iron and a three-wood. 'Those are the only clubs you have left,' Bolt was told.

In the 1960 US Open at Cherry Hills, Bolt went into meltdown on the back nine with a string of bogeys, and worse. At the last, he hooked his drive into a pond, and did exactly the same with his next attempt. 'Teeth bared in crazed rage,' wrote Robert Sommers, 'he drew back his driver with a perfect pivot and exceptionally fine hand position at the top of the backswing, took one step forward,

TOMMY BOLT

and while Claude Harmon, his playing partner, ducked out of the way, he flung his driver into the pond.' A small boy then dived into the pond and retrieved the club, to great applause and even a smile from Bolt at the prospect of the club being returned. But the boy sprinted past Bolt, across the fairway and over a fence, disappearing with his treasure.

Bolt joined the PGA tour aged 34. At one point he was in the army and stationed at a golf club in Rome offering instruction to officers and perfecting his game. He played in two Ryder Cups, including at Lindrick in 1957 when the home side claimed a rare victory. Bolt faced another fiery character, Scotland's Eric Brown, in the singles and when neither appeared on the tee, Jimmy Demaret quipped they were still on the practice range throwing clubs at each other from 50 paces. It was a match full of needle, Bolt losing 4 and 3. He said he did not enjoy the game. Brown said: 'That's because you don't like getting stuffed.'

MICKEY WRIGHT

Born February 14, 1935, San Diego, California
US Open champion 1958, '59, '61 and '64;
LPGA champion 1958, '60, '61 and '63;
Titleholders champion 1961 and '62;
Western Open champion 1962, '63 and '66

Mickey Wright never played golf in Britain, so for golf writers like Liz Kahn and Pat Ward-Thomas even catching a glimpse late in her career was a blessing. 'Meeting Mickey and seeing her play was a highlight in my life,' said Kahn. Ward-Thomas wrote: 'From the moment she stood to the ball there was an impression of authority seen only in the finest men.' Wright had the power of Babe Zaharias but was the total opposite as a personality, far more in the modest mould of Joyce Wethered. Wright and Wethered are contenders – for many the only contenders – for the greatest woman golfer of all time.

MICKEY WRIGHT

Byron Nelson and Ben Hogan said Wright's swing was the best they had ever seen. Herb Warren Wind described her as a 'tall, good-looking girl who struck the ball with the same decisive hand action that the best men players use, her swing like Hogan's in that all the unfunctional [sic.] moves had been pared away, and like Jones's in that its cohesive timing disguised the effort that went into it.'

Like Hogan, Wright was a perfectionist, even well before she turned professional. She had a drive to win like another southern Californian, Tiger Woods. Like Wethered, Jones and Nelson, she had an intense period of winning and then backed away from full-time golf. Her four US Opens has only been matched by Betsy Rawls, her four LPGA Championships is still a record, and her 13 majors second only to Patty Berg. In 1961 she won three majors in the season and two years later she won a record 13 times. She won 81 times between 1956–69, then just once more.

It was advice from Rawls that turned a player with a superior swing who won regularly into a superstar who could not lose. 'Betsy taught me the most important thing of all – to take responsibility for everything that happens to you on a golf course, not to blame the greens for bad putting, the caddie for bad club selection or the fates for a bad day.'

Publicly, Wright spoke out against the prize funds in men's golf, not because she wanted paying more but because 'it is self evident that there is something wrong when a golfer makes $20,000 for a weekend of work, while a professor or scientist can't make that in a couple of years. It seems like a phoney value system to me.' She agreed with an LPGA proposal to cut the first-place prize money and pay out more to players down the leaderboard, which could only adversely affect her.

Wright attracted attention to women's golf not only by her personality but also by the sheer quality of her play. Judy Rankin said: 'She made the golfing world sit up and take notice, and when they started looking past her they saw us. We went from strength to strength thanks to her amazing skills.' All the more remarkable since the men's game had produced another big three, perhaps the biggest trio of all, in Palmer, Nicklaus and Player.

ARNOLD PALMER

Born September 10, 1929, Latrobe, Pennsylvania
**US Amateur champion 1954; Masters champion 1958, '60, '62
and '64; US Open champion 1960; Open champion 1961 and '62**

No one was more exciting than Arnold Palmer on a golf course. Others, before and since, played 'smash it, find it, smash it again' golf but Palmer brought the everyman's charm to what in America was still an elite sport. 'Palmer went after the ball like a guy beating a carpet,' said sports columnist Jim Murray. Legendary US golf writer Dan Jenkins wrote: 'He first came to golf as a muscular young man who could not keep his shirt tail in, who smoked a lot, perspired a lot, and who hit the ball with all of the finesse of a dock worker lifting a crate of auto parts. He made birdies by streaks in his eccentric way – driving through forests, lacing hooks around sharp corners, spewing wild slices over prodigious hills, and then, all hunched up and pigeon-toed, staring putts into the cups. But he made just as many bogeys in his stubborn way.'

Palmer learnt the game at the nine-hole Latrobe, where his father, Deke, was greenkeeper and professional. Deke told his son to get the grip right and then hit the ball hard. With huge shoulders, thick forearms and strong hands, Arnie hit it hard. Balanced and effortless, it was not. But he simply loved to play, and the passion has never dimmed, whether in public or with friends at home. Most of all, he looked everyone in the eye and smiled, spent hours signing autographs. His fans on the course were the adoring Arnie's Army, while millions more watched at home. When he was not playing, he was piloting his jet to the next event.

With great good fortune for the game, Palmer's greatest triumphs arrived shortly after television started broadcasting golf. Today's golfers make millions because of 'Mr. Palmer', while Mark McCormack founded a mighty sports promotion agency, the International Management Group, based on a simple handshake with him.

The first televised Masters was in 1956. By 1964 Palmer was the first player to win four green jackets. In 1960 he birdied the last two holes to win. At the next major, the US Open, he came

ARNOLD PALMER

from seven behind at Cherry Hills, driving the first green at the par-four first hole on the way to a 65. He arrived at the Centenary Open hoping to emulate Bobby Jones's Grand Slam but was just beaten by Kel Nagle.

He would return to win the Open in the next two years, and America, then the centre of the game, once more took notice of the oldest championship. He never did win the USPGA and there were losses galore, not least when Jack Nicklaus arrived, but it all added to the attraction. Jenkins again: 'He is the most immeasurable of all golf champions. But this is not entirely true because of all he has won, or because of that mysterious fury with which he has managed to rally himself. It is partly because of the nobility he has brought to losing. And more than anything, it is true because of the pure, unmixed joy he has brought to trying.'

JACK NICKLAUS

Born January 21, 1940, Columbus, Ohio
US Amateur champion 1959 and '61;
US Open champion 1962, '67, '72 and '80;
Masters champion 1963, '65, '66, '72, '75 and '86;
USPGA champion 1963, '71, '73, '75 and '80;
Open champion 1966, '70 and '78

If Arnold Palmer played competitive golf for longer than anyone, Jack Nicklaus won for longer than anyone. Henry Longhurst was 'very surprised' Nicklaus turned professional at the end of 1961. With two US Amateurs to his name, a lucrative career selling insurance awaited. But with Palmer and television, for the first time a golf career could also be lucrative. It was championships, though, not riches that Nicklaus aimed for. Longhurst added: 'How will Nicklaus fare in direct competition with Palmer? I think very well. Firstly, let me go on record as saying that, like Palmer, he is not only a fine golfer but a very fine fellow. He looks the world in the eye with a fearless sincerity and he has "guts".'

For his first professional win, Nicklaus beat Palmer in a play-off at the 1962 US Open at Oakmont. 'He's got everything,' Palmer said. 'You'll be reading about tournaments he's won for a lot of years.' In 1986 Nicklaus won a record sixth green jacket in one of the most exciting, unexpected and joyous Masters of all (though his fifth, 11 years earlier, against Johnny Miller and Tom Weiskopf at their best, was another of the most stirring championships). Nicklaus collected 18 professional major titles, while the next best is Tiger Woods, stuck on 14 despite his avowed quest to get to 19. Amazingly, Nicklaus was also second in 19 majors and finished in the top five on 19 other occasions. He hung around the leaderboard at majors, often playing conservatively but with the aim of 'playing my own game longer than the rest of them could play theirs'.

Palmer loved to play, Gary Player was all dedication but no one exhibited more concentration and determination than Nicklaus. He was a powerful striker, hitting wondrous long-irons. His swing was honed by Jack Grout, who would stand in front of him and hold his blond locks. 'I learned not to move my head if I wanted to keep my hair,' Nicklaus said. Although a relatively poor chipper and bunker player, only Woods (maybe) ranks with Nicklaus as a pressure putter. Bobby Jones said: 'He plays a game with which I am not familiar.'

The longevity of his winning may be down to his stoic acceptance of losing. Henry Cotton once asked Nicklaus why he did not win more. 'Don't forget, Henry,' Nicklaus replied, 'I am human.' He also played relatively few tournaments. 'I was as fresh at the end of a year as at the start.' But, more than anything, there was his wife, Barbara, and their family, as well as his interests in hunting and fishing, tennis and boating, and then a golf course design business. Pat Ward-Thomas went out sailing with Nicklaus and wrote: 'He seemed absolutely identified with the ocean and boat, standing easily as it bucked over the waves. Golf was in another world; it could never be an obsession with him; he has always had the priceless gift of detachment. Never has the ancient phrase about a healthy mind in a healthy body been more true of a golfer than it is of Jack Nicklaus.'

JACK NICKLAUS

GARY PLAYER

Born November 1, 1935, Johannesburg, South Africa
Open champion 1959, '68 and '74; Masters champion 1961, '74 and '78; USPGA champion 1962 and '72; US Open champion 1965

Gary Player won nine major championships and at the 1965 US Open he became only the third player to win all four majors, joining Gene Sarazen and Ben Hogan. He beat the might of American golf, the likes of Arnold Palmer, Jack Nicklaus and Lee Trevino. But he was not of American golf. He was a South African, of short and slight stature, who overcame a dodgy swing and the necessity to travel halfway around the world to achieve anything (his 13 South African Open titles aside). Some years ago it was said he had clocked up over 13 million air miles in golf's cause. 'He works hard, he out-travels Magellan, and there's never been a tougher competitor,' wrote Dan Jenkins.

But with Player it was never just about the golf. In 2000 he was named South Africa's greatest ever athlete but he was also named among the top five of his nation's most influential people. Once a defender of apartheid, he later denounced it and named Nelson Mandela as his hero. Mandela wrote in *Golf Digest*: 'Few men in our country's history did as much to enact political changes for the better that eventually improved the lives of millions of his countrymen. Through his tremendous influence as a great athlete, Mr. Player accomplished what many politicians could not. And he did it with courage, perseverance, patience, pride, understanding and dignity that would have been extraordinary even for a world leader.'

At the 1969 USPGA, anti-apartheid protesters dogged his every move, threw ice in his face and tried to charge him on a green. He still finished second. He was always a good man in a crisis. In fact, a crisis saw him at his best, whether in a bunker – he became the very best recovery artist from sand – or starting the final round of the 1978 Masters seven behind but coming home in 30 to equal the course record of 64 and win a third green jacket. Or being seven-down after 19 holes to Tony Lema in the World Match Play. He won that match at the 37th and the title five times.

His first golfing crisis came on his first trip to Britain in 1955. He barely broke even and the locals were not impressed. Peter Alliss was among those who thought Player should return home and play golf only socially. 'He had a hooker's grip and a very flat swing,' Alliss said. 'Worse, he had little balance or rhythm and no apparent feel for the game. We perhaps didn't notice his tenacity and how good he was around the greens.'

Player has spoken at length about fitness – he was the first to exercise other than on the course or in the bar – religion, diet, drugs, obesity and the like. He coined his famous phrase: 'It is truly amazing, the more I practise, the luckier I get.' He also said: 'Look after your body. If you do, it could last you a lifetime.' Not everyone has always been impressed. US Ryder Cup player Dave Hill quipped: 'So what if he has the most perfect bowel movement on tour?'

JULIUS BOROS

Born March 3, 1920, Fairfield, Connecticut;
died May 28, 1994, Fort Lauderdale, Florida
US Open champion 1952 and '63; USPGA champion 1968

Gary Player won his last big title aged 42, yet this ranks low on the table of oldest major champions. Jack Nicklaus and Old Tom Morris were both 46 but Julius Boros was 48 when he won the 1968 USPGA by one stroke from Arnold Palmer and Jacky Cupit. According to Dan Jenkins, 'a middle-aged man struck a blow for tired, portly, beer-drinking, slow-moving fathers of seven. Julius Boros, who is all of those things, says he doesn't so much play spectacular golf as "throw a lot of junk up in the air".' Some junk. Lee Trevino said Boros could hit drives 'down those turnpike tunnels and not hit either side'.

By game and temperament he was suited to the US Open, which he won twice. Trevino added: 'When he putts you can't tell by looking whether he's just practising or that it's 50 grand if he sinks it.' Boros disputed the impression. 'I was as apprehensive as the next guy in a tight situation,' he admitted. 'It felt like razor blades in my stomach.'

'Julius never looks like he's playing for anything but self-punishment,' wrote Jenkins at the 1968 USPGA. 'He wastes no time. He strolls up and slaps the ball, and good or bad, he walks away expressionless. He smokes and stands under an umbrella, shielding himself from the heat, and yearns for a cold beer.'

Boros, of Hungarian heritage, was known as 'Moose' by his peers. He turned professional at the age of 29, the end of a career for some players. He was an accountant who had a heart problem which was discovered when he was in the army. But he played lots of golf and was tutored by Tommy Armour. Armour was of the hit-at-it-hard school. Boros did the opposite – his mantra was 'swing easy to hit hard'. He feared locking up over the ball so he would walk up to it, shuffle his feet into position and then swing right away. It was said he was the slowest to get to a ball, but the quickest once he was there. He had a great short game. Armour's advice on turning professional was to 'aim for the bunkers and you might make it'. Within three years he had beaten Ben Hogan, then in his pomp, to win the 1952 US Open.

Form came and went but Boros kept on playing and contending into his 50s, more than once having a chance to beat Sam Snead's record as the oldest winner on the PGA Tour at 52. He played a part in the creation of the Seniors (now Champions) Tour and when asked if he would ever retire, he replied: 'Retire to what? All I know how to do is play golf and fish.' He died of a heart attack playing at Coral Ridge in 1994. Two years later his son Guy also became a winner on the PGA Tour at the Greater Vancouver Open.

TONY LEMA

Born February 25, 1934, Oakland, California;
died July 24, 1966, Lansing, Illinois
Open champion 1964

Tony Lema, like Julius Boros, was a late starter but, unlike Boros, his career ended suddenly at its peak when he was killed in a plane crash at the age of 32. A marine in Korea before becom-

JULIUS BOROS

TONY LEMA

ing an assistant pro in San Francisco, he was encouraged by Eddie Lowery, the one-time caddie of 1913 US Open champion Francis Ouimet. His first few years on tour were not successful but he got there in the end. He won his first tournament, the Orange County Open, in 1962. After the third round, Lema promised the press they would all celebrate with champagne. The next day he beat Bob Rosburg in a playoff and made good on his promise. He was ever after known as 'Champagne Tony' and then celebrated all his wins the same way. The odd enlightened champion still continues the tradition today.

Lema said in his first few years on tour he 'moved from city to city like a zombie'. But he came to enjoy the high life, such a contrast to the poverty of his childhood. A tall, handsome man, he was popular with both players and spectators. He had an elegant swing, all rhythm and grace, and was a superb pitcher to the green. In 1963 he was runner-up to Jack Nicklaus at the Masters. In 1964 he had won four tournaments, including three in four weeks, prior to arriving at the Open at St. Andrews.

Arnold Palmer did not make the trip that year so told Lema to secure the services of the caddie who had helped him to a runner-up finish and two victories in the previous four years. Tip Anderson, a St. Andrews legend, guided Lema around the Old Course, which was vital since the American only arrived 36 hours prior to the first round and had only one practice round. So well did Lema execute Anderson's instructions that he beat Nicklaus by five strokes. 'It was without doubt one of the most remarkable victories in the championship's history,' wrote Peter Ryde. 'He showed rare judgement and control of the little shots into the greens which have no parallel in America, putted marvellously on greens which had baffled many distinguished overseas challengers of the past, and drove superbly – particularly on the first day when gale-force gusts blew from the west.'

Lema had quickly established himself as one of the next rung below the Big Three. A brave defence of his Open title was only thwarted at the end by Peter Thomson. In two Ryder Cup appearances, he lost only one of 11 games. After the 1966 USPGA, Lema, then aged 32, and his wife Betty and two companions, travelled from Akron, Ohio to Chicago in a private plane which ran out of fuel approaching its destination. The plane crashed on a golf course in Lansing, Illinois, the pilot managing to avoid a crowd of people by the clubhouse. More than a thousand people attended his funeral, with Palmer among the pallbearers.

BILLY CASPER

Born June 24, 1931, San Diego, California
**US Open champion 1959 and '66;
Masters champion 1970**

Put-downs of Billy Casper are legion. 'An empty car drove up to the clubhouse and Billy Casper got out,' was one. Another: 'He is so austere in his personal life that by contrast a Franciscan monk looks like a swinger.' Dave Hill, always ready with a quip about his fellow players, said: 'He has as much personality as a glass of water.' At the 1959 US Open, when Casper had 31 single-putt greens but made only eight birdies, Dan Jenkins wrote: 'For four rounds he escaped from more dangers than Tarzan. The only thing he didn't do was swing from a vine to save par.'

There was no need, since Casper could save par with his deadly putting. He had an unusually wristy action but it was highly effective. 'Billy has the greatest pair of hands God ever gave a human being,' said Johnny Miller. Casper won three majors and 51 times on the PGA Tour playing against the Big Three and the rest. He plotted his way around the course with the sort of intensity Ben Hogan used to have. It was a deliberate act of homage to his hero. 'Hogan seemed to be in this sort of hypnotic state, and I wanted to be just as focused,' Casper explained.

The only time the rotund Casper got serious ink from the press was when he complained about his allergies or went on a diet of buffalo, elk and bear meat, giving rise to his nickname 'Buffalo Billy'. He is a Mormon and has 11 children, six adopted. Miller called Casper the 'most underrated golfer of all time, hands down.'

BILLY CASPER

'Billy was a killer on the golf course,' said Dave Marr. 'He just gave you this terrible feeling he was never going to make a mistake, and then of course he'd drive that stake through your heart with that putter. It was a very efficient operation.' The most famous example came at Olympic in the 1966 US Open. Everyone wanted Arnold Palmer to win and he led Casper by seven strokes with nine holes to play but Palmer collapsed, Casper came home in 32 and the pair tied. In the playoff, Palmer led by four at the turn but, yet again, Casper rallied to become the villain of the piece. 'I had seen other guys tense up, panic under pressure, but not Arnie,' Casper said. 'His swing just got shorter and faster.'

'To be a winner you have to have heart,' said Jack Nicklaus. 'You really have to control your emotions and your golf game. Billy Casper was wonderful at this and does not get the credit he deserves. He didn't have all the shots that others had but he was able to will the ball into the hole.'

He was not one for worrying about technique. 'How does a seagull fly? How does a centipede get all those legs working at once? I've been playing this game of golf for more than 20 years. I just do it. I don't question it.'

BOB CHARLES

Born March 14, 1936, Auckland, New Zealand
Open champion 1963

B ob Charles ranked alongside Billy Casper and Bobby Locke as one of the great putters in the game. He remains New Zealand's greatest ever player. And he was the finest left-hander the world had then seen. Harry Vardon may never have seen a left-hander 'worth a damn' but Charles was the first to win a major and the only one until Mike Weir and Phil Mickelson. Charles is right-handed in everything but games requiring two hands. His parents played left-handed and so he merely picked up some of their spare clubs. His success and endorsements of left-handed clubs helped make the game more accessible for those who play the 'wrong way round'.

Charles was a different sort of putter to Casper. A tall man, he played much more in the modern way, keeping the wrist out of it and hinging from the shoulders. He seemed to hole everything from inside five feet and a three-putt was a rarity indeed. His greatest triumph was a good example. After a long amateur career when he was also a bank teller, Charles turned professional in 1960 and just three years later he won the Open at Royal Lytham. He beat Phil Rodgers in the last ever 36-hole playoff by eight strokes and in the morning round alone single-putted 11 times. 'When he was on the green, the hole was never safe,' reported the *Sunday Telegraph*. 'Keeping his wrists unbroken and moving the club-head more slowly under pressure than the game's case-hardened chroniclers had ever seen, Charles dropped putt after putt from any distance.'

On the 30th anniversary of his victory, Charles returned to Lytham and won the Senior Open Championship for the second time with a birdie on the last hole. *Golf Weekly* said: 'If you had to put your life on someone sinking the winning putt in a major that someone would be Charles. When it comes to testing seven-footers there is no-one better.'

Charles was never a flamboyant player. 'I'm an introvert,' he admitted. 'I take things seriously, particularly my golf. That's my business and the golf course is my office.' But he won events all around the world, including the World Match Play at Wentworth in 1969, the year he was runner-up in the Open for the second successive year. He won in Japan, South Africa and Europe, as well as on the PGA Tour in America and was even more successful on the Champions Tour. In 2007 he set a record as the oldest player to make the cut in a non-seniors event. Aged 71 he was invited to play in the centenary New Zealand Open, which he had won for the first of four times as an 18-year-old amateur in 1954. After an opening 75, Charles scored a 68 on Friday to make the cut. He matched his age with a 71 on Saturday and then broke his age again with a 70 on Sunday and received a standing ovation at the final hole. He was awarded a knighthood in 1999.

Bob Charles

ROBERTO DE VICENZO

Born April 14, 1923, Buenos Aires, Argentina
Open champion 1967

The best of times and the worst of times, as far as championship golf goes, arrived for Roberto de Vicenzo within a nine-month stretch. When he won the Open in 1967, it was joy unconfined but the 1968 Masters was one of the saddest of climaxes to any major. De Vincenzo was a charming man and became South America's greatest player, despite starting in the game as a caddie's assistant – fetching balls from positions where no self-respecting caddie would dream of prostrating himself. But he grew strong and tall and developed the most pleasing swing. He was a peerless ballstriker and despite an unreliable putter, won around 200 times around the world.

When he first played at the Open in 1948, Bernard Darwin said he gave 'more aesthetic pleasure than any other man in the field'. He finished third for the first of five times and was second in 1950, so by the time he played at Hoylake in 1967, he was the sentimental favourite. Jack Nicklaus put the pressure on by birdying two of the last three holes but de Vicenzo hit a superb wood over the corner of the practice field (out of bounds) to the green at the par-five 16th and victory was assured. 'Vicenzo, the look of an emperor about him, strode into the amphitheatre by the last green towards a reception the like of which I had never heard before,' wrote Pat Ward-Thomas. 'Its sustained warmth and affection were tribute to a fine human being as well as to a great golfer and a victory nobly won.'

He was 44 at the time of his greatest victory. His 45th birthday was on Easter Day 1968, the final round of the Masters. De Vicenzo holed a full nine-iron for an eagle at the first hole and the gallery serenaded him with a burst of 'Happy Birthday'. He birdied the next two holes and a three at the 17th seemed to assure victory. But he bogeyed the last and then failed to notice that his playing partner, Tommy Aaron, had put down a four for the 17th instead of a three. The error came to light too late and the four had to stand.

ROBERTO DE VICENZO

Instead of a 65, he was given a 66 and lost by one to Bob Goalby. The scene was one of distress but, famously, de Vicenzo said: 'What a stupid I am.'

Ward-Thomas recalled his appearance in the interview room. 'He sat on the dais, for all the world like a great wounded bear, and faced a barrage of questions, many of them uninformed and inconsiderate and designed to snare him into criticising others, but he steadfastly insisted that the fault was his alone.' Arguably Goalby was the more affected and he never received his due as a major champion. Some time later, the Golf Writers Association of America presented de Vicenzo with its award for sportsmanship. He looked at the trophy and said: 'Golf writers make three mistakes spelling my name on trophy. Maybe I not the only stupid.'

CATHERINE LACOSTE

Born June 27, 1945, Paris, France
US Women's Open champion 1967;
British Ladies Amateur champion 1969;
US Women's Amateur champion 1969

Catherine Lacoste never had a professional golf career. She hardly had a career in golf at all. She was a shooting star so glorious as never to be forgotten. It was as if, having emerged from the shadow of her parents with her own momentous achievements, she was happy to do other things, get married, start a family, run the golf club started by her grandfather at Chantaco and serve on the board of the famous family clothing business. At the age of 22 Lacoste was then the youngest ever winner of the US Women's Open and she remains the only amateur to win the title. 'It made me into a person who wasn't just my parents' daughter,' she said.

She had impeccable sporting genes. Her father was René Lacoste, the great French tennis player, a multiple grand slam champion and one of the 'Three Musketeers' along with Henri Cochet and Jean

CATHERINE LACOSTE

Borotra. Her mother was Simone Thion de la Chaume, who won the British Ladies Amateur in 1927 and was the greatest French player of her era, competing against the likes of Cecil Leitch and Glenna Collett. Catherine said she was a lousy tennis player but she rode, played handball, volleyball and basketball, yet excelled at golf. She had some lessons from the great Jean Garaialde but otherwise developed her game playing in little tournaments organised by her mother at Chantaco.

In 1964 Lacoste led France to victory in the inaugural Espirito Santo Trophy in Paris, and two years later she won the Astor Trophy with a round of 66 at Prince's that was considered one of the finest rounds ever played by a woman. Yet she was unheralded when she travelled alone to Hot Springs, Virginia, and led from start to finish against the might of the American tour to win the US Women's Open. Two years later she won her own grand slam, the Amateur titles of Spain, France and the two that had eluded her so far, the two she most wanted, the British and American championships.

'She was sparky, cheery and talented,' recalled Peter Alliss. She was as powerful a striker of a one-iron as the women's game has known. She could also be 'scornful of opposition to the point of giving offence,' wrote golf journalist Peter Ryde. 'Add to this some blunt remarks, remarkable more for their honesty than for their tact, and it is hardly surprising that she roused occasional animosity. She once admitted to being perhaps "*un peu cabochard*". We must make what we can of that, but "*caboche*" is a hob-nail, and riding roughshod over people's feelings might not be wide of the mark.'

Yet there was an awareness of what a competitive life might cost. 'Each time you win, you lose a little of your sensitivity. And that's a bad thing for a girl,' she said. Even in her prime, Lacoste admitted she found too much golf boring. 'I think golf should be fun,' she said, 'and I wouldn't have much fun as a pro.'

JoAnne Carner

Born April 4, 1939, Kirkland, Washington
US Women's Amateur champion 1957, '60, '62, '66 and '68;
US Women's Open champion 1971 and '76

JoAnne Carner had a 'presence that was completely overwhelming', said Peter Alliss. 'She had a wonderfully slow, hippy, rhythmical walk. She smoked, but she didn't just smoke, she smoked as dramatically and as stylishly as Ingrid Bergman or Dean Martin. She liked a glass of beer, too, and had a wonderfully open face framed by short, fair, curly hair, a broad mouth, strong teeth and a ready smile, the look of someone you could completely trust in whatever situation you found yourself in.'

As JoAnne Gunderson, Carner emerged from the Pacific Northwest to win the US Amateur five times, one fewer than the record held by Glenna Collett Vare. Twice she faced Marlene Stewart Streit in the final, losing one and winning one. The 'Great Gundy' loved head-to-head competition and never lost a singles in the Curtis Cup.

At the age of 24, she married Don Carner. He was much older, the owner of an electronics and jewellery business. 'There are two things we don't discuss,' Don Carner said, 'JoAnne's weight and my age.' They were inseparable, living in a trailer which they drove from event to event, setting up never far from fertile fishing waters. In 1969 Carner won an event on the LPGA circuit. It was the moment that persuaded her to turn professional but while she thought she would dominate immediately, and she won the first of her US Open crowns in 1971, it took a few years. In 1974 she won six times, and then the victories kept coming.

'I expected to take over the tour but Sandra Haynie told me it would take four years,' Carner recalled. 'I said, baloney, but it did. I was used to matchplay and winning, not staying there and grinding it out for $500.' She was a strong driver of the ball. Sandra Palmer said the 'ground shakes when she hit it' and not for nothing did her new nickname become 'Big Momma'. Advice from Billy Martin, the manager of the New York Yankees, was the key. 'He told me not to analyse what I was doing with every club on the practice tee before I played. He said I should use that time strictly as a warm up session to loosen the muscles. His advice made me stop over-analysing and work out my problems after the round.'

She added: 'I have never had any trouble controlling my emotions. I get excited with pressure, not nervous, and you have to learn how to compensate when you are pumped up. But I can't play if I get too serious. I relieve the pressure with a little light chatter with the gallery. I enjoy my golf more than anyone.' At one point Carner was the LPGA's leading money winner of all time but money is a warped currency in evaluating success. In 1981 Carner was involved in a race to become the first woman to win over $1 million. She was pipped by someone who had started earning and winning a decade earlier, Kathy Whitworth.

KATHY WHITWORTH

Born September 27, 1939, Monahans, Texas
Titleholders champion 1965 and '66; LPGA champion 1967, '71 and '75; Western Open champion 1967

It was with a certain irony that Kathy Whitworth's career earnings went past $1 million at the 1981 US Women's Open. It was the one title she never won, and the one that meant most to her. 'I would have swapped being the first to make a million for winning the Open,' she said, 'but it was a consolation which took some of the sting out of not winning.'

In a later era, Karrie Webb became the first player to win $1 million in an LPGA season. But many of Whitworth's records still stand. She won a tournament each season for 17 consecutive years and in 22 seasons in all. Her most famous record is her 88 career victories. In the 1980s, amidst much publicity, she first overtook the 82 of Mickey Wright and then the 84 of Sam Snead – his USPGA Tour record was later downgraded to match Wright's 82. Whitworth's first win was in 1962. She won six major titles including three LPGA Championships, and her last regular win came in 1985.

The following year was a financial disaster when the management company to which she had entrusted her savings filed for bankruptcy. 'It was very depressing, a sickening feeling that is hard to describe,' she told Liz Kahn. 'You can't believe it is happening to you. After the initial shock, I realised I was young enough to get a job and make some money. I couldn't really cry because compared to many older people who lost everything, it was not nearly so brutal for me. You can wallow in it and not accomplish anything, or you can go on.' She became a teaching professional and, in particular, helped young women from Japan become professionals themselves.

Whitworth grew up in New Mexico but when she showed talent, her local pro drove her down to Austin to learn from Harvey Penick. Her first few years on tour were unsuccessful. Tall and striking, she was also painfully shy but she was taken under the wing of Wright and Betsy Rawls. She worshipped Wright but competing against her brought out the best in Whitworth. Always modest, Whitworth never rated her own swing but Penick put her at the top of his list when someone needed to hole a long, crucial putt. She was a 'feel' putter who thought only of making a good stroke, not whether or not it would go in. 'At her peak, she would get a mental picture of the line of the putt, and her hands would control the distance,' said Penick. 'Putting was as simple as pointing her finger.'

Whitworth said: 'I was fortunate to be so successful. What I did being a better player does not make me a better person. I am not smarter or more intelligent than someone who digs a good ditch. When I'm asked how I would like to be remembered, I feel that if people remember me at all it will be good enough.'

JoAnne Carner

Kathy Whitworth

CHARLIE SIFFORD

Born June 2, 1922, Charlotte, North Carolina

John Shippen finished sixth at the second US Open in 1896 but it took an intervention from USGA president Theodore Havemeyer, who had donated the trophy the year before, to prevent a boycott by white players at the inclusion of black player Shippen and Native American Oscar Bunn. When the PGA of America was formed in 1916, the constitution stated that members had to be of the Caucasian race. This was only removed in 1961 after the state attorney of California threatened to ban the tour from holding events in his state. Charlie Sifford had become the first black player to gain his PGA card the previous year.

Bill Spiller and Ted Rhodes were two of the most prominent pioneers before Sifford, who had started in the game by caddying. After serving in the army, Sifford won the National Negro Open, run by the United Golf Association, six times and became the personal professional of jazz singer and band leader Billy Eckstine. Sifford provided coaching and Eckstine helped fund Sifford's travels to those tournaments on the PGA Tour that did not discriminate. 'To have a man like Mr B behind me was the most wonderful thing that ever happened to me,' said Sifford, whom Eckstine called 'Little Horse'. 'He was the benefactor who made it possible for me to live my dream.'

In the *History of the PGA Tour*, Al Barkow wrote: 'Sifford had a gruff and sometimes difficult manner, but he was not a radical in the way that Jackie Robinson was in breaking baseball's colour barrier. The NAACP wanted Sifford to challenge sponsors who would not let him play, mainly in the southern states, but Sifford wouldn't. And in those places where he played and was subjected to racial insults, he turned his cheek or withdrew from the tourney. Nonetheless, Sifford put himself out there, took the abuse when it came – and it did come – and kept going. In all, he was a solid frontiersman for his race.'

Sifford was in his late 30s when he was first allowed to play full-time on tour, but he won twice, at the 1967 Hartford Open

CHARLIE SIFFORD

and the 1969 Los Angeles Open. 'If you try hard enough,' he said, 'anything can happen.' He never played in the Masters, however. That distinction went to Lee Elder after he won the Monsanto Open in 1974. Elder was present at Augusta when Tiger Woods won in 1997. Tiger said of Sifford: 'He has my respect and my gratitude for the sacrifices he made to open the doors to this great game to people of colour.'

Sifford won the 1975 PGA Senior Championship and also won on the Seniors Tour in its inaugural year of 1980. His autobiography, published in 1992, was called *Just Let Me Play*. In 2004 he was inducted into the World Golf Hall of Fame in the lifetime achievement category. 'Man, I'm in the World Hall of Fame,' he said at the induction ceremony. 'That little old golf I played was all right, wasn't it?'

THE NICKLAUS
CHALLENGERS
1970–1980

While Jack Nicklaus remained the man to beat, a few great champions emerged as the heirs to the Bear. They were the men who took on the best player in the game and won – like Lee Trevino, who grew up knowing what it was like playing for a sum of money greater than that which he could afford to pay should he lose. He rarely lost. And he often beat Nicklaus, as did Tom Watson. Thought of as a choker after his early efforts in majors fell short, Watson went on to win eight majors titles, including a famous victory against Nicklaus in the Duel in the Sun at Turnberry in 1977.

Other pretenders to Nicklaus' crown emerged as the world's leading golfers strove to achieve dominance. Johnny Miller was briefly the best player on the planet, but did not last at the top, as Raymond Floyd did, after settling down as a family man. For one glorious year, Tony Jacklin vanquished all-comers to win both the Open and then the US Open. Later he would be the guiding force behind Europe's rise to Ryder Cup triumph.

While the men's game sought its new Nicklaus, the women's game found its Palmer in Nancy Lopez, who became the darling of the fans, her dazzling smile and attractive personality bringing much-needed attention to the LPGA.

Lee Trevino

LEE TREVINO

Born December 1, 1939, Dallas, Texas
US Open champion 1968 and '71;
Open champion 1971 and '72;
USPGA 1974 and '84

Tony Jacklin once made a simple request of Lee Trevino. 'Lee, is it okay if we don't talk today?' Jacklin said. 'Sure, Tony,' came the reply. 'You don't have to talk, just listen.' Chatter was all part of the act for Trevino. It was his way of dealing with the nerves but his concentration over the ball was total. Few could flick the switch like that. Few played golf like Trevino. He won six majors and survived being hit by lightning. He used to say: 'In case of lightning, walk down the middle of the fairway and hold your one-iron over your head. Even God can't hit a one-iron.' Later, he said: 'When God wants to play through, you let Him.'

It was Trevino who said: 'Pressure? Pressure is playing for $5 when you only have $2 in your pocket.' He grew up in poverty in Dallas and never knew his father. After serving in the US Marines, he became an assistant pro in El Paso. He made money playing against anyone who would take him on. Ray Floyd, already a star by then, once arrived and was surprised to be playing the locker-room attendant who collected his clubs from his car. It was a three-day match and Floyd only just won, Trevino having had the better of the first day rounds. Floyd told his fellow tour players: 'Boys, there's a little Mexican kid out in El Paso. When he comes out here, you'll have to make way for him.'

Few may have believed him. Trevino's flat, lunging swing did not inspire confidence, according to Peter Dobereiner. 'He gave the impression of a man who was not so much interested in practising his golf as working off some deep grudge against the balls. He was punishing them. Or, more accurately, he was identifying the balls with people and getting his own back.' Somehow he sliced the ball with a hooker's grip but the swing repeated, even under pressure.

Trevino was fifth at the US Open in 1967 and became the Rookie of the Year but a year later his wife had to stake his entrance fee.

Trevino was the first player to score four rounds under 70 in a major and he beat Jack Nicklaus into second place. He did that four times in majors, greatness making way for greatness. At Merion in 1971 he beat Nicklaus in a playoff and he ended up with the US, Canadian and British Open titles within weeks.

At Muirfield a year later, Nicklaus was trying to become the first player to hold all four major titles at once. He finished strongly to set the target but Trevino and Jacklin were a shot ahead playing the par-five 17th. Trevino was in trouble, still off the green in four, while Jacklin had a 15-footer for a birdie. Super Mex seemed almost disinterested when he walked up to his ball but chipped in and went berserk. Jacklin three-putted. Trevino hit two great shots at the last and was champion again. Jacklin never was.

TONY JACKLIN

Born July 7, 1944, Scunthorpe, Lincolnshire
Open champion 1969; US Open champion 1970

Tony Jacklin said about the 1972 Open: 'The heart was ripped out of me. I stepped off the 18th green a shattered man, broken by what had happened. I was honestly never the same again.' Jacklin's success had come so swiftly that perhaps there was no foundation for dealing with such a setback. 'Was he just a firework?' asked Henry Cotton. 'Well, there's no doubt for a brief period Jacklin was a sensational golfer.'

Jacklin was the most exciting thing to happen to British golf for decades. The son of a Scunthorpe steelworker, his game developed under a hard taskmaster, the Australian Bill Shankland at Potters Bar. He was a product of his time. Ben Wright recalled him turning up for an interview in 'gold lamé pants, gold cashmere sweater over a white polo neck and gold shoes. I thought, well, that's great, this kid really believes in himself.' In 1968 Jacklin was the first Briton to win on the modern PGA Tour. A year later at Lytham he ended another of those Open droughts for home champions, dating back

to Max Faulkner in 1951. A slower rhythm to his swing was the key and he drove superbly, especially at the last – 'What a corker!' gasped Henry Longhurst on television. 'So smoothly was Jacklin swinging, so true was his striking and so confident the stride of his jaunty figure that it seemed impossible for him to fail,' wrote Pat Ward-Thomas.

In 1970 Jacklin became the first Briton, excluding those naturalised Americans, to win the US Open for 50 years, and Harry Vardon is the only other British golfer to have held the US and British titles simultaneously. At Hazeltine, an immature Minnesotan course, Jacklin survived a week of gales to win by seven strokes. On the last morning Tom Weiskopf left a one-word message in Jacklin's locker: 'tempo'. At the age of 25 Jacklin was on top of the world. After 1972, there were wins, including a second British PGA title in 1982, but he rarely again challenged at the highest level and he retired relatively early.

But he will ever be associated with the Ryder Cup. As a player, he was involved in the famous match in 1969 when Jack Nicklaus conceded him a short putt for a win on the last green that meant the match was tied (and America retained). Nicklaus said to Jacklin: 'I didn't think you were going to miss but I wasn't going to give you the chance.' Many years later the pair built a golf course they named 'The Concession'. Jacklin became an inspirational European captain in 1983, demanding cashmere and Concorde for his players and getting the best out of Seve Ballesteros and Europe's other emerging stars, with historic victories at the Belfry in 1985 and Muirfield Village, Nicklaus's own course, in 1987. 'Jacklin had three great gifts,' wrote David Davies, 'a magnificent golf game when wholly interested in the project at hand, a superb talent for captaincy and an unerring instinct for getting up people's noses. He is beyond doubt the best captain the Ryder Cup has seen.'

RAYMOND FLOYD

Born September 4, 1942, Fort Bragg, North Carolina
USPGA champion 1969 and '82; Masters champion 1976;
US Open champion 1986

When Ray Floyd brought out 'The Stare', then beware. Floyd was from the Hogan school of golf. Jolly, he was not. Even in a practice round, there had to be something on it; dollars were exchanged. In competition, he had an intense focus that helped him hole putts under pressure. 'When he gets that look in his eyes,' said Lanny Wadkins, 'he's hard to handle.' His wife, Maria, said: 'I've seen Raymond win without it, but I've never seen him lose with it. I know then they are going to have to beat him, he's not going to falter.'

Meeting Maria and getting married were the pivotal moments in Floyd's career which saw him win on the PGA Tour from 1963 until 1992, the year he became the first player to win on both the regular and senior circuits in the same season. Floyd started hitting balls aged four at the driving range owned by his father, a former military man. Once he began competing, he quickly became a winner on tour but other delights of the lifestyle appealed more. 'Winning tournaments meant nothing to me,' he said. 'I thought the tour was just one big ball, travelling from Miami to Los Angeles to New York and all those other exciting places.'

He added: 'I don't really care what people think about my lifestyle. I'm a bachelor and if it makes me a playboy to be seen with a different girl every now and then so be it. I can't see me finishing 18 holes and hurrying back to the motel to practise putting on the rug.'

But becoming a family man changed everything, although not until after quitting one tournament mid-round in 1974 and skulking in a hotel room for two days. 'Maria jumped on me like a tiger,' Floyd said. 'It helped put my life in proper focus. From that moment on, I was a more mature, patient and responsible man.'

Floyd had won the 1969 USPGA, but he won three more majors and many more regular events in the second part of his career. In 1976 he won the Masters by eight strokes, equalling Jack Nicklaus's then record score. He used a five-wood for approaches at the par-

Raymond Floyd

fives and was 14 under for those 16 holes. Ten years later, Floyd won the US Open at Shinnecock Hills by two from Wadkins. Even then, there were bombers and shot-makers and 'Tempo Raymondo' and Wadkins were in the second camp. Wadkins said at the start of that week: 'This course ought to reward golf shots and guys like myself and Raymond are among the few people out here who can make our four-irons talk.'

Floyd lost a playoff for the 1990 Masters to Nick Faldo and was second to Fred Couples two years later. It was playing with the competitive Floyd in the 1991 Ryder Cup that helped the laidback Couples become a champion. In 1993 Floyd was picked at the age of 51 for his 'heart and guts', said captain Tom Watson.

JOHNNY MILLER

Born April 29, 1947, San Francisco, California
US Open champion 1973; Open champion 1976

'There is no better way to become an overnight, instant, presto matinee idol in golf,' wrote Dan Jenkins, 'than to put yourself somewhere back in the Allegheny hills – about 12 coal mines and six roadhouses behind everybody trying to win the 1973 US Open, including a modest cast of Jack Nicklaus, Lee Trevino, Arnold Palmer, Gary Player, Julius Boros and Tom Weiskopf – and come cruising along with your blond mane flapping in the breeze, young, handsome, trim and knock them all sideways with a sizzling round of golf that you've somehow pulled out of nowhere.'

For a brief period, Johnny Miller was the best player in the world. He had been a prodigy ever since finishing eighth as an amateur in the 1966 US Open, or perhaps since his father started calling him 'Champ'. But in 1973, Miller produced his record 63 at Oakmont, perhaps the least forgiving course in America. It was a sensation. 'What the hell is Miller doing?' Palmer asked his playing partner after looking at the leaderboard. 'I didn't even know Miller made the cut,' said Weiskopf.

Johnny Miller

Miller won eight times in 1974 and four times in 1975, the year he and Weiskopf pushed Nicklaus all the way at the Masters. Miller hit his irons superbly. At the time, no one hit the ball closer to the hole so consistently. 'When I get going it's like I'm in a trance,' he said. 'I know what's going on around me but I can black everything out. It's like I'm hypnotised. I can see things that are going to happen. I feel like I'm going to birdie every hole. It was sort of golfing nirvana. I'd say my average iron shot for three months in 1975 was within five feet of my line, and I had the means for controlling distance. I could feel the shot so well.' At Birkdale in 1976, Miller scored a 66 in the final round to beat the 19-year-old Seve Ballesteros. The Spaniard's career was just getting going, Miller never won another major, and did not win a regular event for four years.

Like Ray Floyd, once he became a family man, his priorities changed. But unlike Floyd, his golf suffered. He worked hard on his ranch and his body got stronger but he lost the feel in his swing. He suffered from the 'yips'. The ambition was no longer there. 'When I got to the mountaintop, I kind of looked at the scenery and wondered, "Now what?" When Jack got there, he said, "Where's the next mountain?"'

Miller took up television commentary in the 1990s and proved popular with viewers, less so with players since he was not afraid to criticise. But in 1994 he entered the AT&T National Pro-Am at Pebble Beach and beat Tom Watson and Tom Kite for the title. 'This isn't right, this is a fluke,' he said. 'I'm not a golfer, I'm a television announcer. I'm a grandfather for crying out loud.'

HALE IRWIN

Born June 3, 1945, Joplin, Missouri
US Open champion 1974, '79 and '90

Hale Irwin was the perfect US Open player, calm and focussed, but even he could not keep his emotions in check at all times. When he holed a big, breaking putt from over 45 feet at the 72nd hole at Medinah in 1990, he did something very un-Irwin-like. He set off running around the green, like a 'possessed teenager at a disco,' someone said, slapping hands with the entire front row of the gallery. Irwin was 45 and had never before expressed such emotion on the golf course. He ended up in a playoff with Mike Donald and the next day Irwin won it at the 91st hole to become the oldest winner of America's national championship. Dan Jenkins wrote: 'It's worth noting that Hale became the only guy ever to win US Opens wearing glasses (1974), braces on his teeth (1979), and contact lenses (1990).'

'The thing that triggered it,' Irwin said of his celebratory scamper, 'was the volume of noise. When I looked over and saw the crowd going wild, I got caught up in the excitement and my instinct was to share it with them. It changed how the world looked at me.'

Irwin was known for playing gridiron football in college, playing well on tough courses, winning US Opens and hitting memorable two-irons under pressure. Excitement, he was not known for. He played alongside Seve Ballesteros for the last two rounds and it made quite a contrast. Irwin could not believe someone could be so wild off the tee and still win. 'I don't know what image is,' Irwin said. 'I suppose it's some sort of chemistry or style. Some people have it, some don't. Palmer was interesting because he was so aggressive, free-wheeling, a hitter. So is Ballesteros. He'll hit it over any lake on the golf course because the public comes to see him do it.'

Irwin won what was called the 'Massacre at Winged Foot' in 1974 with a score of seven over par. It was the year Sandy Tatum, chairman of the USGA's championship committee, said: 'We're not trying to embarrass the best players in the world, we're trying to identify them.' Of his college football career, Irwin said: 'I was undersized, under speed, under everything. But I had the determination to get it done. The intensity that I had to play at allowed me to compete with others with better skills.' When he got out on the golf tour, he said: 'I relished the harder courses because I just felt I was going to try harder.'

Irwin remains the most successful winner on the Champions Tour and in 1997, despite the disparity in prize money, he won more on his circuit than Tiger Woods did for topping the money list on the

HALE IRWIN

regular tour. He won two World Match Plays at Wentworth but is remembered for missing a tap-in putt, literally of two inches with the putter hitting the ground and bouncing over the ball, during the third round of the 1983 Open. He lost by one to Tom Watson the next day.

TOM WATSON

Born September 4, 1949, Kansas City, Missouri
Open champion 1975, '77, '80, '82 and '83;
Masters champion 1977 and '81; US Open champion 1982

When it comes to a late, romantic, major win, nothing, not even Jack Nicklaus at the 1986 Masters, would have compared with Tom Watson winning the Open in 2009 at Turnberry. At the age of 59. Feeling a sense of spirituality and living off the memories of 1977, he birdied the 17th as he had 32 years earlier. No one dared believe it would happen until he marched down the 18th fairway like the Watson of old, victory within reach. And that's when it went wrong. An approach over the green, a bobbled putt up the bank, a dribbled championship putt from eight feet that exposed an old Watson. A crushing sense of deflation and anti-climax hung over the playoff, won admirably by Stewart Cink. 'It would have been a hell of a story, wouldn't it?' Watson said. 'It wasn't to be. It tears at your gut, as it has always torn at my gut. The dream almost came true. Almost.' Looking around at his inconsolable listeners, he added: 'This ain't a funeral, you know.'

There was a time when the man from Kansas City, via Stanford University, made 'Watson pars', scrambling from everywhere, ramming in putts or making the one back if necessary. He might have matched Harry Vardon's record of six Open titles at St. Andrews in 1984 but for overcooking his second at the 17th and losing to Seve Ballesteros. Ironically, it was only after he had won three times that Watson truly fell in love with links golf, having been educated in the art by his friend Sandy Tatum on trips to the likes of Ballybunion

TOM WATSON

and Dornoch, in all weathers, a simple pencil bag over the shoulder. 'He has a real reverence for the game, which adds to the distinctive quality to watching him play,' Tatum said. 'Verve, heart, intelligence and imagination are characteristics that have added so much to his career.'

In the late 1970s and early 1980s he was the best player around, notably defeating Nicklaus at the 1977 Masters and then again at that summer's Open at Turnberry. They played together for the last two rounds: Watson 65, 65; Nicklaus 65, 66. It was the 'Duel in the Sun' and on the last day Watson holed a huge putt at the 15th to get level, birdied the 17th and hit a sublime seven-iron to two feet at the last. Nicklaus was in a bush off the last tee but smashed it onto the green and holed his own monster putt. Suddenly Watson's putt was no longer a gimme, but he holed out anyway. They left the green arm-in-arm. 'I'm tired of giving it my best shot and coming up short,' Nicklaus told the champion. Hubert Green was third, 11 strokes back.

Then, at the 1982 US Open, Watson chipped in, improbably, from thick rough for a birdie at the 17th and beat Nicklaus again. Nicklaus told him: 'You little son-of-a-bitch, you're something else. I'm proud of you.' Watson had seen a leaderboard on the 17th and thought: 'It's just me and Nicklaus, and I always beat Nicklaus.' Few thought that, fewer did it.

NANCY LOPEZ

Born January 6, 1957, Torrance, California
LPGA champion 1978, '85 and '89

The fairytale ending to Nancy Lopez's career would have been to win the US Women's Open in 1997 but instead she finished as runner-up for the fourth time. The first time she had been an 18-year-old amateur in 1975. Now she was 40 and a hero to the players she was competing against, not least the champion, England's Alison Nicholas, who knew full well her greatest triumph also had

NANCY LOPEZ

her pegged as public enemy number one. 'I'd love to have won the Open,' Lopez said. 'But I've had enough good things in life that I won't be shattered because I don't.'

Lopez grew up in Roswell, New Mexico, and was a sensation when she turned professional. She won nine times in her rookie season in 1978, including the first of three LPGA Championships. It was a streak of five victories in a row that made her a star to the wider world. The next year she won eight times. 'They have the wrong person playing Wonder Woman,' said Judy Rankin. Mickey Wright said: 'Never in my life have I seen such control from someone so young.'

Her effect on the woman's game was like of that Arnold Palmer on the men's game in the 1960s. Lopez's appeal was far more than simply being a fierce competitor. 'She is a physically appealing woman, with dark hair, brown eyes and a warm, dazzling smile. She was God's gift to the LPGA,' wrote Liz Kahn. Dottie Pepper said: 'As good as Nancy has been on the course, she has been even better off the course. There is something very genuine about her. Nancy, like Arnold Palmer, related to people. She didn't just relate to the gallery, she related to her competitors. She beat you but she beat you with a smile on her face.'

Inevitably, she could not keep winning at the same rate. But she determined that however she played, she would keep on smiling and not hide from the attentions of media or fans. 'It is always hard to put on a public face and sometimes I want to freak out, but it is important to me to keep a good image. My image reflects on me, my husband, my family, my life. Everyone should be good in public.'

Lopez, whose mother died young, also said: 'Before I was what I am now, I wasn't anything. I wanted to win for my parents because they sacrificed a lot for me to play golf. They were always there when I needed them and I wanted them to be proud of me. I couldn't do anything except play golf to repay them.' She married for the second time to baseball star Ray Knight and they have three daughters. Two of her three majors arrived after becoming a mother. 'I've never felt a career is more important than a family, or life in general. Some professional athletes are so tied up with themselves they forget what got them there. I want to be remembered as a person who appreciated what was done for me.'

ISAO AOKI

Born August 31, 1942, Abiko, Chiba, Japan

'He's the Arnold Palmer of Japanese golf,' said Greg Norman when he introduced Isao Aoki at the 2004 induction ceremony for the World Golf Hall of Fame. 'To travel from your home shores, where the culture is different, the language is different, is not an easy task.' Aoki was the first player from his country not just to travel around the world but also to do so successfully. It was watching Palmer on television that spurred him to travel. 'He was my idol,' Aoki said. 'My dream was to see the world.'

No Japanese player has come closer to winning a major championship than Aoki, at the US Open at Baltusrol in 1980. Aoki broke the record for the championship's four-round total but, alas, so did Jack Nicklaus, who won by two strokes. Although Aoki had won the World Match Play at Wentworth in 1978, and was runner-up the following year, he was not well known in America. For US observers, his novel putting style was a surprise.

Despite being over six feet tall – he was nicknamed 'Tower' after the Tokyo Tower – he once used a putter whose shaft was too long for him. So he pushed the clubhead as far away as possible, meaning the toe of the putter lifted into the air and he hit right on the heel. The putter may have been discarded but the style remained a lifelong success. Dan Jenkins noted: 'Aoki would have looked like the best clown act in town, except the ball kept going into the hole.' Both players birdied the last two holes, both par-fives, and that Nicklaus had had to work so hard was part of the satisfaction of winning a fourth US Open. 'I kept telling myself no matter how perfect he is, he will make a mistake in 72 holes in four days,' Aoki said. 'But I was wrong.'

Aoki won in Japan for over two decades but his best year was in 1983 when he won the Hawaiian Open, the European Open at Sunningdale and his first Japan Open. He was the first Japanese to win on both the US and European tours. Sometimes, he did not need his famous putting. In the World Match Play in 1979 he holed in one at the second hole, winning a holiday home at Gleneagles, and

Isao Aoki

he won the '83 Hawaiian Open by holing a wedge shot from 128 yards for an eagle.

Aoki went on to have success on the Champions Tour in America and is a familiar figure as a commentator for Japanese television. In 2011 he was joined in the World Golf Hall of Fame by Masashi 'Jumbo' Ozaki, one of three golfing brothers and Japan's most prolific winner with over a hundred domestic victories but only one overseas, in New Zealand. While Ryo Ishikawa, a teenage star, may develop into his country's finest player, it is Aoki who has led the way. 'He's influenced all the modern day Japanese players,' said Larry Nelson. 'They've gotten better and better since he started playing and winning outside his country.'

Seve and the
rise of Europe
1980–1995

For over 60 years, America had dominated the world of golf. Now the fight back was on and it was led by Seve Ballesteros. Seve just oozed charisma and his dashing play, both erratic and blessed with genius, inspired many across Europe to fall in love with the game. He led the way and his peers, Bernhard Langer, Sandy Lyle, Nick Faldo and Ian Woosnam, all followed. Augusta National, that very American citadel, fell to the European invaders year after year and once the Big Five all had a green jacket (or more than one), along came José María Olazábal, Seve's equally talented Ryder Cup partner. Under the captaincy of Tony Jacklin, Europe beat the Americans and turned the match from something of an American victory procession into the keenly contested event that we know today. Others who came through this European nursery of great talent, before settling in America, were Australia's Greg Norman and Zimbabwe's Nick Price. Curtis Strange became the best of the Americans, twice winning the US Open and only just failing in his hat-trick bid.

SEVERIANO BALLESTEROS

Born April 9, 1957, Pedreña, Spain;
died May 7, 2011, Pedreña, Spain

Open champion 1979, '84 and '88; Masters champion 1980 and '83

'Severiano Ballesteros,' wrote David Davies, 'is unquestionably the finest, greatest thing ever to happen to European golf. No golfer has ever made more impact on a whole continent than the dashing, crashing Spaniard: Seve of silken swing; Seve slash-and-burn; Seve of the Spanish Main, sword in teeth, carrying off the crinolined crumpet.'

Ballesteros was the first, both by birth date and deed, of a group of five European golfers born within a year of each other. 'Lyle, Langer, Woosie and Faldo were the players in seats 1A, 1B, 1C and 1D,' said Ken Brown. 'But none of them was the pilot flying Concorde. Seve was the pilot.' He made 'Seve fans' of people who knew nothing of golf. He was the Arnold Palmer of Europe. 'But it does Seve Ballesteros a disservice to compare him to anyone. He was unique. He was Seve,' added Brown. Nick Faldo said: 'Seve was golf's *Cirque du Soleil*. The passion, artistry, skill, drama, that was Seve.'

He was wild and brilliant by turns. He hit the ball hard, found it, and did whatever was needed to escape. In his pomp he did not drive the ball as poorly as imagined, and as back trouble made inevitable later. But at Lytham in 1979 he won the Open without troubling many fairways. 'The dust of that brutal assault has not yet settled,' wrote Peter Dobereiner. 'It will take a while for the spectators of the violence to recover. We are dazed like witnesses to a nearby explosion – not a scratch on us but the medics know that we are candidates for a cup of sweet tea and a quiet lie down.'

Seve greeted opponents thus: 'I look into their eyes, shake their hand, pat their back, and wish them luck, but I am thinking, "I am going to bury you".' He took on shots no one else would play. Brown said: 'He had the confidence and the sheer audacity to take on the course in a new way. The rest of us didn't have the skill, or the power, or the balls. Some of us, all three.' His three-wood from a bunker, sliced from 245 yards in the 1983 Ryder Cup was the

SEVERIANO BALLESTEROS

greatest shot Jack Nicklaus said he had ever seen.

Nowhere was better suited to Seve's style than Augusta National. He won two Masters, but he should have won more, not least against Nicklaus in 1986. He felt most loved in Britain. His joyous celebration on the final green at St. Andrews in 1984 became a lasting image, but there were also dark moods, controversy and ructions with officials on both sides of the Atlantic. A passion for beating the Americans drove his Ryder Cup exploits and he formed a stupendous partnership with compatriot José María Olazábal. They had 'no sorries'. Ollie said: 'When Seve gets his Porsche going not even San Pedro in heaven could stop him.' Diagnosed with a brain tumour in 2008, he faced the operations and treatment, and ultimate defeat, the same way he did his golf. He always believed in *'destino'*.

BERNHARD LANGER

Born August 27, 1957, Anhausen, Germany
Masters champion 1985 and '93

Colin Montgomerie tells the tale that could define Bernhard Langer's approach to golf. Langer is all about attention to detail. It is improbable that Langer would need Monty to tell him a yardage but presumably he was merely double-checking when he asked the Scot what was the distance stated on a sprinkler head. Told the number, he then followed up by asking his Ryder Cup partner: 'Is that from the front of the sprinkler head or the back?' Montgomerie shakes his head at that. 'That's Bernhard,' he said.

Langer, the son of a Czech who escaped a Siberia-bound prisoner of war train in 1945, is a man of patience and perseverance, of a strong Christian faith and an unshakeable resolve. He has won more tournaments on the European Tour than anyone bar Seve Ballesteros but his greatest win possibly came in the German Masters in 1991 in a playoff. Little remarkable about that except that the previous Sunday Langer experienced something that might have crushed a lesser golfer.

The 1991 Ryder Cup at Kiawah Island had come down to the last putt of the last hole of the last match. Langer had six feet and two spike marks to negotiate and did not hole it, giving victory to America. 'To some there was a quality so raw and cruel in the circumstances of the US victory as to leave a residue of hollow sadness,' wrote Thomas Boswell. Ballesteros said: 'No one in the world could have holed that putt. Not Jack Nicklaus, or Tony Jacklin and certainly not me.' Langer kept his composure that night until Seve consoled him. Once Seve started crying, Langer could not hold back his own tears.

Langer is the most marvellous middle-iron player but his putting always lacked consistency. Three times he battled back from the yips, often career-ending for others, yet on two occasions he mastered the lethal greens at Augusta. Both his green jackets were won on Easter Sunday. He tried putting crosshanded, then moved his left hand down the shaft and clamped his forearm to the shaft with his right hand, then tried the long putter. 'I don't care what it looks like,' he said. 'We don't get paid for looking good.'

He also said: 'It really doesn't matter if a putt goes in. To me, what matters is that I give the whole subject over to God. I just say: 'If you want me to make this putt or win this tournament then it will happen', if not he has other plans for me. Good things can come out of everything. When you go through bad times, good can follow, because you learn more in bad times than in good times.'

Langer never won the Open despite a number of chances. But he claimed the British Senior Open Championship at Carnoustie in 2010, and won the US Senior Open the very next week in Seattle, another remarkable fortnight in the life of a remarkable German.

SANDY LYLE

Born February 9, 1958, Shrewsbury, Shropshire
Open champion 1985; Masters champion 1988

The day after Sandy Lyle won the Open, he threw a party where he spent most of the time either collecting trays and trays of Chinese food or doing the washing up. The year after he won the

BERNHARD LANGER

SANDY LYLE

Masters, he served up haggis at the Champions' Dinner. 'Everybody had some on their plate,' he said, 'but most of it stayed on the plate.' Lyle was one of the best players in the world and, although his form did not last, he has always been one of the most loved.

He grew up at Hawkstone Park, the son of a Scottish professional, and developed naturally from hitting ball after ball. He and Seve Ballesteros were kindred spirits. Seve once said Lyle was the 'greatest God-given talent in history. If everyone in the world was playing their best, Sandy would win and I'd come second.' There was never the driven ambition of a Nick Faldo. Peter Alliss said: 'Sandy goes along in a world of unconscious competence.'

When it came to hitting a one-iron he was better than competent; only Jack Nicklaus was in the same bracket. On the dangerous 14th hole at Sandwich, after getting into trouble off the tee, Lyle smashed a two-iron onto the green and holed from 40 feet for a birdie-four. It propelled him into contention and despite fluffing a chip in Duncan's Hollow by the 18th green, he became the first British winner of the Open since Tony Jacklin in 1969. Not even Seve could have been a more popular champion

Three years later Lyle was in a bunker off the 18th tee at Augusta yet hit a seven-iron onto the green. Herb Warren Wind called it the greatest bunker shot in the history of golf. 'A sharp cry of admiration arose for this brave and wonderful stroke,' wrote golf writer Cal Brown, 'and then a stunning silence spread through the gallery as the import of the shot registered.' Lyle holed the putt, danced a little jig and started Britain's four-year reign at the Masters.

Yet Lyle's form did not last. Strange to think he never played in the Ryder Cup after the heroics at Muirfield Village in 1987. What had come so naturally, now could not be fixed by the game's great instructors. This became the enduring contrast with Faldo. Up until then, Lyle had always had the upper hand. David Davies wrote: 'Lyle dominated as if by right at every level he experienced right up to the very heights of the game; Faldo had to grind away, experimenting, adapting, adopting, learning things that Lyle had absorbed as a child. Lyle was long, Faldo was not. Lyle ambled amiably round the course, chatting about this and that; Faldo, needing to concentrate all his efforts and energies on golf, was dour and uncommunicative. For a man with an ambition that burned as brightly as did Faldo's it was galling in the extreme to be beaten so often by such a seemingly casual talent.'

SIR NICK FALDO

Born July 18, 1957, Welwyn Garden City, Hertfordshire
Open champion 1987, '90 and '92;
Masters champion 1989, '90 and '96

The perfectionism of Nick Faldo was obvious to everyone; the passion for the game that lay behind it less so, particularly if the end result was not up to standard. 'Everyone suffers on a Faldo round, Faldo most of all,' Brough Scott wrote. 'Anything less than perfection gets a terrible black mark. Out on the course it will never be easy to love him. For he does not love himself.'

Penetrating the Faldo bubble was hard and his attempts to engage, the Norman Wisdom fake trips or the cringing rendition of 'My Way' after winning the 1992 Open, were often misguided. Instead, Faldo's passion for the game comes out far more in his television commentary, or his commitment to junior golf with the Faldo Series, or simply talking about his practice regime or his course design work. Days after visiting his newly seeded Chart Hills course in Kent, I was wandering around Crans-sur-Sierre on pro-am day when from a distant tee the knight-to-be's voice echoed around the mountain tops. 'What did you think of my baby?' he was desperate to know.

Faldo was always sporty but at first he ran, he swam and he cycled. Then he saw Jack Nicklaus on television playing at the Masters and was hooked. To a schools career officer who suggested only one in 10,000 make it in top class sport, he replied: 'Well, I'll be that one, then.' With his height, his swing was always elegant but he thought it was not good enough. With David Leadbetter he took two years to remodel it. He became less handsy and relied more on the bigger muscles of the body, building a swing that was less

SIR NICK FALDO

likely to break down under pressure. His decision to tamper to such an extent was not always applauded or thought necessary but the proof of the pudding came in the eating. Six major titles were sweet indeed. At the very least, he had gone through a Hoganesque process whereby after so much hard work, confidence crowded out any lingering doubts. To express his flair for the game, he needed such strong foundations. He dealt in precise subtleties, fading or drawing an approach to the yard, with or against the wind, using the contours of the ground, which drew admiration while Seve and Sandy produced flamboyant escapes, generating affection.

He did whatever it took, like making 18 successive pars to win at Muirfield in 1987. Twice he took on Greg Norman and defeated the Shark, in the third round at St. Andrews in 1990, leading to a carefree crowning the following day, and, unforgettably and remorselessly, from six strokes behind at Augusta in 1996, Faldo relentlessly forcing Norman's greatest ever collapse. 'Don't let the beggars get you down,' Faldo told Norman as they embraced at the 18th. Notorious were the battles Faldo had with the press down the years. But leading British sports writer Hugh McIlvanney wrote: 'There was in the years of his prime something quietly beautiful about the relentless, slow-burning courage with which he played golf. His balls were unbreakable. Among British sportsmen, Nick Faldo ranks with the greatest of the great.'

IAN WOOSNAM

Born March 2, 1958, Oswestry, Shropshire
Masters champion 1991

After Sandy Lyle handed the green jacket to Nick Faldo, who put it on himself as only the second person to successfully defend at the Masters, Faldo then handed it on to Ian Woosnam. Wee Woosie was the youngest, shortest and latest developer of Europe's Big Five but his place among them, suggested by his tour victories and his record in the Ryder Cup, where he shared a formidable partnership with Faldo at one point, was confirmed with his triumph at Augusta. At the 18th he smashed his drive way over the bunkers on the left and had only a short pitch from the midst of the gallery to the green, where he holed a Woosie-length putt, as David Davies described it, meaning one of around five feet, four inches. Earlier Woosnam had been heckled something rotten. 'Hey, you're not on no links course here,' he was told. Woosie, the farmer's son whose strength came from lugging bales of hay, only bristled more. Tom Watson, his playing partner, told him how Don January would turn to the gallery in such circumstances and very politely say, 'F... you very much.'

Around that time, Augusta always seemed to come up with the best player in the world, whether Ballesteros, Langer, Lyle, Faldo or Fred Couples in 1992. In 1991 it was Woosnam. His first big year had been 1987 when he won the World Cup with David Llewellyn for Wales and was also the first British winner of the World Match Play. In succession he beat Faldo, Ballesteros and Lyle, all on the 36th green. Like Lyle, Woosnam grew up in Shropshire but took the country of his parents, rightly so since he learned his golf at Llanymynech, which has 15 holes in Wales and only three in England. At a Hereford Boys event, Woosnam lost to Lyle and said: 'One day I'll beat you.' Lyle replied: 'You'll have to grow a bit first, Woosie.' After the 1987 World Match Play, Lyle added: 'If he ever grows up, he'll hit the ball 2,000 yards.'

Woosnam hit the ball huge distances with one of the sweetest swings in the business, his only thought to 'turn and swish'. 'There's nothing mechanical about Woosnam at all,' said Jack Nicklaus. 'He's about as smooth and flowing a player as I've seen.' John Jacobs, the master coach, said: 'For me Ian Woosnam swings the club exactly the way I think it should be swung. He is the perfect exemplar of the secret of long hitting – clubhead speed correctly applied.'

His swing took him from a camper van and a diet of baked beans, to owning his own private jet. An unreliable putter stopped him achieving even more. He once said: 'I became the best in the world and I thought I had to change everything to stay the best. I tried to change my swing and that was a load of rubbish. I went to a sports psychologist and that was a load of crap. I'm a natural.'

Ian Woosnam

Curtis Strange

CURTIS STRANGE

Born January 30, 1955, Norfolk, Virginia
US Open champion 1988 and '89

Nick Faldo and Ian Woosnam might have added to their major tallies but for Curtis Strange. In the late 1980s Strange fought an almost single-handed rearguard action against the rise of European golf. He was three times the leading money winner on the PGA Tour and suffered disaster in the creek at the 13th at Augusta to lose the 1985 Masters to Bernhard Langer. He was a grinder and it was his quest for a hat-trick of US Open titles that came to define his career. At Brookline in 1988 he got up and down from a bunker at the last hole to tie Faldo and then won the playoff comfortably. He said: 'It means what every little boy dreams about when he plays by himself late in the afternoon. He has three or four balls; one's Hogan, one's Palmer, one's Nicklaus and one's Strange; 99 per cent of the time those dreams don't come true.'

A year later at Oak Hill, Strange won again and Woosnam was one of the runners-up. Not since Ben Hogan in 1951 had someone won back-to-back titles. Only Willie Anderson at the start of the century had won three in a row. All his efforts and all the focus were on his attempt to match Anderson at Medinah. A 68 in the third round put him in contention but a 75 on the final day left him in 21st place. 'I could never have imagined the feeling I had leaving Medinah that day,' Strange admitted. 'I've never quite found the right words to describe it – the wind went out of my sails like never before in my life and it lasted a long, long time. When you drive and work so hard to do something ... disappointment is the wrong word, it's just a letdown.'

Strange never again won a tournament. He had always played with what was described as a 'barely controlled rage' and he was often fined for the sort of industrial language that any hacker might use about their own golf. After Medinah, it all got too much. He suffered from headaches and lethargy and the intensity seeped from his game. 'Maybe I lost enthusiasm because I knew my game was going south. I couldn't stop it for a while. The pressure to play well every day was part of it. We only have so much energy, mentally and physically, to be the best. The first thing that goes is the mental edge. Except for Jack Nicklaus, it's only for seven or eight years.'

One regret he later admitted to was not travelling to the Open Championship in some of his best years. Typically, the more people said he should go, the more he resisted. When he became a television commentator he interviewed Tiger Woods at his first event as a professional in 1996. When Woods said he expected to win every time he teed up, Strange laughed and said: 'You'll learn.' Woods won his fifth start as a professional and kept on winning.

BEN CRENSHAW

Born January 11, 1952, Austin, Texas
Masters champion 1984 and '95

Harvey Penick, a publishing phenomenon in his ninth decade with his *Little Red Book*, told his pupils, whether on the tee or the green, to 'take dead aim'. As for putting, he believed the younger Willie Park had it right that a 'man who can putt is a match for anyone'. Penick believed in 'dying' the ball into the hole so as to 'give luck a chance'. He died, aged 90, on the Sunday before the 1995 Masters. Two weeks earlier he had given Ben Crenshaw his last putting lesson: 'Take two practice strokes on the green before you putt. Don't let the head of the club pass your hands on the stroke.' On the day before the Masters, Crenshaw, the 1984 Masters champion, Tom Kite, the 1992 US Open champion, and Davis Love, soon to be the 1997 USPGA champion, flew to Austin to attend Penick's funeral. The following Sunday Crenshaw won, without three-putting once, and Love was second. Crenshaw doubled over in grief on the 18th green. 'I had a 15th club in the bag and it was Harvey,' he said. 'It was like someone had their hand on my shoulder this week and guided me through.'

Penick had first placed a club in Crenshaw's hands when he was eight. Crenshaw and Kite, who both grew up and remained in Austin, were his favourite pupils. Kite said he never saw Crenshaw

miss a putt from the age of 12 until he was 20. When he was 15 Crenshaw's father gave him a putter christened 'Little Ben'. It turned out to be a faithful servant. 'I leaned on that putter hard to bail me out,' Crenshaw said. 'It did some extraordinary things.' But it was not always well treated. 'We're going to get you for child abuse, you treat him so poorly,' Dave Marr told him. Crenshaw's nickname of 'Gentle Ben' proves Americans can do irony.

After a fine amateur career he became a favourite on tour but he had to wait a decade, and suffer five runner-up finishes, before his first major at the age of 32. 'You could have watered all the botanical wonders on the course with the tears of joy that were creeping down the cheeks of the thousands whose hopes he had crushed so often,' wrote Dan Jenkins. Crenshaw, a golf historian as well as a noted course architect, said: 'I could give you a million reasons why I love Augusta; why it's as exciting as your first date, as exhilarating as a ride on a giant wooden roller coaster and as comfortable as an old shoe.'

Crenshaw was the Ryder Cup captain in 1999 at Brookline. The Americans trailed by four points on the Saturday night but Crenshaw said: 'I'm a big believer in fate. I have a good feeling about this. That's all I'm going to say.' The following day the America won the singles by 8½ points to 3½, the biggest comeback ever in the event. Passions turned to anger among the Europeans, however, when the Americans celebrated on the 17th green before José María Olazábal had a chance to putt.

PAYNE STEWART

Born January 30, 1957, Springfield, Missouri;
died October 25, 1999, Aberdeen, South Dakota
USPGA champion 1989; US Open champion 1991 and '99

Tony Lema was 32 when he died in a plane crash. Payne Stewart was 42 when he too perished in a private jet. Four months earlier he had won the US Open for the second time but his concern had been for Phil Mickelson, the runner-up, whose wife was due to give birth for the first time. Stewart told him: 'You'll win the Open but now you have more important things to do. You'll be a great daddy.' At that year's Ryder Cup at Brookline, Stewart had a spectator who heckled his singles opponent, Colin Montgomerie, ejected and ultimately conceded the match once America had won and pandemonium had broken out. Montgomerie carried a photograph from that day in his business folder. 'Every time I pull it out I think back to the moment Payne gave me the match and how fragile life can be,' he said.

At Stewart's funeral, Paul Azinger said: 'For many years it seemed like Payne Stewart was first in Payne Stewart's life. But not long ago this began to change. We saw a man as interested in people as in golf. A man who played to win but truly loved others at the same time.'

Stewart was a brash American who wore his trademark plus-fours, for many years in the colours of the local NFL team where the tournament was taking place. He had a graceful swing and a touch to his short game that helped him prosper on British links. He was twice second at the Open and would prepare for his trips to Britain by visiting Ireland. 'If I ran for mayor in Waterville it would be a landslide,' he said. 'I don't know why they have accepted me so much but we have a very good time. We get into the pub, get round the piano and I bring out the harmonica and before you know, it's about four in the morning.' His early career saw him play all round the world in order to establish himself, and in Kuala Lumpur he met his Australian wife Tracey. Two major titles did little to change him but his two children did. 'This walk I am having in Christianity is being led by my children,' he said.

Stewart was twice runner-up to Lee Janzen at the US Open, in 1993 and 1998. 'He's more outgoing than most people on tour,' Janzen said, 'but his style of play is exactly the opposite. Nothing fancy, hit the fairways, hit the greens and try and make a few putts.' At Pinehurst a year later Stewart holed vital putts down the stretch, including from 15 feet for a par at the last. He vanquished Mickelson, Woods, Singh and Duval, with Stewart a worthy champion.

PAYNE STEWART

On October 25, he, his three colleagues, and the two pilots, died when their Lear 35 private jet lost cabin pressure shortly after take-off from Orlando. The plane continued to fly on autopilot, with all on board almost certainly dead, until it ran out of fuel and crashed into a field in South Dakota.

GREG NORMAN

Born February 10, 1955, Mount Isa, Australia
Open champion 1986 and '93

Somehow Greg Norman won only two majors. Only? More than enough for most but not Norman. Not for the attention he compelled as a golfer and a character. This striking man with a blond mop from Down Under was nicknamed the 'Great White Shark' on his Masters debut in 1981 and, inevitably, it stuck. 'If you wanted to be a golfer, this is the one you'd want to be,' wrote Jim Murray. 'Like a lot of great athletes, energy just seems to radiate out of him. He lashes at the ball as if it were something he caught coming through his bedroom window at two in the morning.'

As a cash generator Norman is in the same league as Arnold Palmer and Tiger Woods. He may be the most successful ever golfer-turned-businessman, with interests in course design and construction, turf licensing, wine, clothing and restaurants. And for much of the 1990s, it seemed, he was number one on the world rankings, his record at the top only overtaken by Woods. Before Butch Harmon coached Woods, Harmon coached Norman and harnessed his massive power so he became the longest, *straightest* driver in the game.

Although so often not the case, at his best Norman did manage to avoid grasping defeat from the jaws of victory. At Royal St. George's in 1993, Norman won his second Open with a 64, the lowest closing score ever to win an Open, to defeat Faldo, Langer, Pavin, Price, Els *et al*. Gene Sarazen, in his last visit to an Open, said: 'This must be the greatest championship ever played. I've never seen such shots.' Norman agreed: 'I never mishit a single

GREG NORMAN

shot. I am in awe of how well I hit the golf ball today.'

Yet Norman became the second man after Craig Wood to lose a playoff at all four majors and in 1986 did the Saturday Slam, leading after 54 holes each time but only winning at Turnberry. He will be remembered as much for the titles he did not win as for those he did. More, maybe. There were cock-ups, approaches blazed way right of the final green, and conspiracy of fate: Bob Tway holed out from a bunker at the 1986 USPGA and Larry Mize chipped in at the second extra hole to win the 1987 Masters. He only came to terms with those two after breaking down in tears in a television interview with former Australian prime minister Bob Hawke in 1992. He almost won the 2008 Open as a 53-year-old but the 1996 Masters was his greatest disaster. Peter Dobereiner, though he regretted it afterwards, told him in the locker room on the Saturday night: 'Not even you could f... this one up.' Norman led by six at the end of the third round but lost by five to an imperious Nick Faldo. 'I'm a winner,' he said, 'just not today. I'm not a loser in life.'

Donald Trump told *Golf Digest*: 'Greg can be controversial, but people who profess to have a problem with him are just jealous. He looks better than they do, he plays better than they do, and he's a better businessman.'

NICK PRICE

Born January 28, 1957, Durban, South Africa
USPGA champion 1992 and '94; Open champion 1994

Nice guys don't come first, unless they are called Nick Price. When he won the 1994 USPGA, Dan Jenkins wrote: 'Nick Price may have three majors now, but that's not the best thing about him. He's as nice a guy as you'll find in the game.' Price disputes the 'nice' tag, but only in the sense that 'I just wish someone would say I'm friendly or warm or however you want to describe me.' Price was born in South Africa of British parents and grew up in what was then Rhodesia. He did his military service at the time of the country's civil war that led to independence. It gave him a perspective on the game he chose to make his profession. 'Military service taught me that golf wasn't the be-all and end-all in life and that I was fortunate to do something I loved,' he said.

His mother asked just one thing of him: 'I don't care how successful you are, what you've done in life, how much money you make – it doesn't matter. All I want to see every time I see you is a smile on your face. Then I know I've done well.' Price learned his lesson well. When the Golf Writers Association of America inaugurated an award in memory of the late *Los Angeles Times* writer Jim Murray to honour a player who, in being approachable and accessible, 'reflects the most positive aspects of the working relationship between athlete and journalist', the first winner was Nick Price; the second was Arnold Palmer.

Price followed the same route as his friend Greg Norman, first playing in Europe, then settling in Florida. For a time in the 1990s the pair dominated the game. Price was always a superb ball-striker but his putting could be variable. He let the Open slip away in 1982 and six years later had it prised away from him by Seve Ballesteros. Finally, he broke through at major level by winning the 1992 USPGA. Two years later he had won the Open and the USPGA back-to-back. His monster putt on the 17th green helped him to victory at Turnberry, while he was magnificent at Southern Hills, five up at halfway and winning by six. Ben Crenshaw said: 'He's a man in full flight. He's striking the ball better than anyone since Hogan and Nelson.' Price said: 'I'd always dreamed of playing that way, and I finally did it at Southern Hills. It was what my journey was all about.'

He shared this journey with Jeff 'Squeaky' Medlen until the caddie died from leukaemia at the age of 43. 'He was diligent and conscientious and humble and simple and honest and all the good things any man should be,' was Price's tribute. Medlen won three USPGAs in all because in 1991 Price withdrew to attend the birth of his first child and loaned his 'looper' to the last player to get into the championship, John Daly.

JOHN DALY

Born April 28, 1966, Carmichael, California
USPGA champion 1991; Open champion 1995

John Daly, an unknown 25-year-old, late of mini-tours and a winter in South Africa, was the ninth alternate for the 1991 USPGA. When Nick Price withdrew, at the last minute, the sixth, seventh and eighth alternates could not make it at such short notice. Daly set off from his home in Memphis on the off-chance, drove for seven hours, and arrived in Indianapolis at midnight to find a message that he was in the field. Without a practice round at Crooked Stick he went round in 69, 67, 69 and 71 and won by three strokes. The course was so long by the standards of the day that David Feherty said it was the first he played 'where you need to take into account the curvature of the earth'. It was perfect for Daly's long-hitting game. He said he just 'gripped it and ripped it'. His caddie, Price's man Squeaky, simply said 'kill' whenever Daly addressed the ball. He took the lead after the second round and never looked back. Hailed as golf's new star, Daly said: 'I'm not gonna become a jerk. If I become a jerk, I'll quit golf.'

Daly has not quit golf yet, it just seems like it at times. Peter Dobereiner wrote in 1995: 'There can be no denying that John Daly has brought the profession of golf into disrepute. Repeatedly so. He has blotted his copybook, let the side down, embarrassed his fellow professionals by making a frightful ass of himself and so on. He has been brought to book, hauled over the coals, put on a fizzer, marched up before the beak, carpeted and castigated and given numerous rockets. He has, one has to admit, accepted his various punishments without demur.' A further decade and a half of misdemeanours can be taken into account.

There have been four divorces – *All my exes wear Rolexes*, he sang – suspensions, overnight stays in jail, visits to rehab, addictions to Jack Daniels – 'I started drinking four years after I started playing golf. And I started playing golf when I was four' – Diet Coke, chocolate chip muffins and gambling, including $1.5 million lost on slot machines in Las Vegas the night after losing a playoff

JOHN DALY

in 2005 to Tiger Woods. In 2009 he had gastric band surgery in order to lose weight and now claims to be more 'Mild Thing' than 'Wild Thing'.

Daly is the only two-time major winner never picked for the Ryder Cup but, at his best, he would have been the ultimate wild card. He had a surprisingly delicate touch to complement his extraordinary length. R&A secretary Michael Bonallack thought Daly might win the 1995 Open on the Old Course and he did, hitting through the wind and laying long approach putts stone dead. Costantino Rocca holed a remarkable 60-foot putt from the Valley of Sin to tie, but Daly won the playoff. Fred Couples said: 'He's one of the few players out there I'd pay to watch. I root for him to win more than I root for me.'

JOSÉ MARÍA OLAZÁBAL

Born February 5, 1966, Fuenterrabía, Spain
Amateur champion 1984; Masters champion 1994 and '99

An announcement of a new Ryder Cup captain always causes a stir. There are always mutterings, but not in the case of José María Olazábal, captain of Europe in the 2012 match in Medinah in the USA. No one, not a single solitary person, had a bad word to say. 'It was probably the easiest decision we've ever had to make,' said Thomas Bjørn. 'He has the passion and the determination that we all associate with the Ryder Cup.' Paul Casey played with Ollie in 2006 and was a player when Olazábal was a vice-captain in 2008. 'He is the only person who has twice reduced me to tears with his speeches,' Casey said. At the 2010 Ryder Cup at Celtic Manor, Olazábal was seconded as an extra assistant by Colin Montgomerie after the Spaniard turned up as a representative of a coffee machine company. 'We thought that was a waste of his expertise, experience and passion,' Monty said.

'The Ryder Cup has been special to me, to my life,' Olazábal said. His debut came in 1987 at Muirfield Village, the start of

José María Olazábal

a partnership with Seve Ballesteros that brought 11 wins and two halves from 15 matches. 'I've won a couple of majors and it is just you and your caddie. When you win the Ryder Cup, the joy is beyond imagination. You are with 11 other players, their wives and girlfriends, all the backroom staff, and there is nothing to compare.'

Blessed with the same skill and imagination around the greens as Ballesteros, he had a fast swing that produced wonderful iron shots but inconsistent driving. He once said at a formal dinner, 'This speech is like my tee shot. I don't know where it's going.' He played with an intensity that brought immediate success in the professional game but also mighty sulks when his form dipped. Mostly it was his manager Sergio Gomez and his wife Maite who had to put up with the tirades, or the sullen silences, which might last an entire flight home from Japan. Early in 1994 Maite read Ollie the riot act. 'You are a disgrace and you will be over as a golfer unless you grow up,' she said. John Jacobs, the famed golf coach, tweaked his swing, or rather 'found the right words' to make Olazábal listen, and that April Olazábal won the Masters. 'Be patient. You have what it takes to win. You are the best in the world,' was the note Ballesteros left for Olazábal before the final round. He became the only post-War winner of the British Amateur to win a professional major.

In 1995 and '96 Olazábal suffered from rheumatoid polyarthritis, which has recurred in recent years. He was not properly diagnosed until he saw Dr Hans-Wilhelm Müller-Wohlfahrt in Munich. He recovered to play under Seve in Spain's Ryder Cup in 1997 and win another green jacket two years later. He recalled: 'In the mornings, to get to the bathroom, it was only nine feet but I could not get there on my feet. I had to crawl. At that point I thought I would end my life in a wheelchair. I did not think I could ever play golf again.'

COLIN MONTGOMERIE
Born June 23, 1963, Glasgow, Lanarkshire

'I'm only here for entertainment value,' said Colin Montgomerie when ushered in front of reporters and television cameras at one US Open. It was probably a day when it was a case of 'I'm not the story', and with Tiger Woods accelerating away from the field he was probably right. But most days he was the story. For a decade and more, Montgomerie propped up European golf, taking the strain between the Big Five and the latest batch of stars, whom Monty captained to victory in the 2010 Ryder Cup. In the Monty era, no one else was anywhere near as quotable, did more, or had more things happen to him.

He won (not just tournaments but an incredible, unlikely to be repeated, seven orders of merit in a row from 1993-99) and he lost, he played sublime golf and he behaved appallingly, berating marshals, cameramen, spectators with crisp packets, butterflies in adjacent fields, anyone, really, who dared to breathe at the wrong moment – it was never going to work with American galleries. In the interview tent he could be charming, or volcanic. In a gale at Carnoustie with the tent rattling as if about to take off, his hair out sideways, a 75 on his scorecard, a daft laddie asked: 'Was the wind a factor?' He could only repeat and repeat the question, his face reddening, the voice rising by the octave, before storming out.

José María Olazábal was an early nemesis, beating Monty in the final of the 1984 Amateur, holing two chips, two bunker shots and a full eight-iron. Then came Ernie Els, who beat him at both the 1994 and '97 US Opens, and Tiger Woods. Monty thought his experience would prevail in the third round of the 1997 Masters. At the end of a dispiriting day, he admitted: 'There is no way humanly possible that Tiger Woods is not going to win.' At St. Andrews in 2005, Monty chased Tiger all the way and at the US Open at Winged Foot the next year his approach came up short and right. He took a six when a four would have done it. No one without a major has suffered as many as his five second places. 'You wonder sometimes,' he said, 'why you put yourself through this.'

Colin Montgomerie

He was the world number two and might have reached the top spot. He was a magnificent putter until he persuaded himself he wasn't. He said of his run as European number one: 'Successful, yes, of course. Happy, no I wasn't. If I'd been overtaken, I would have felt a complete failure.' The Ryder Cup always brought out the best in him. 'And I'm glad it does. My personal record means nothing.' Olazábal said in 1999: 'It looks like we are the average workers and he is the gifted one. He doesn't practise much. He doesn't need to. He keeps hitting the ball straight down the fairway and straight on to the green and scoring well. What can you say?'

THE TIGER ERA
1995–2011

While Colin Montgomerie found Ernie Els something of a nemesis during the 1990s, Els had the misfortune to play some of his best golf just as Tiger Woods arrived. Combining power – thanks, in part, to great athleticism, as well as technological advances in clubs and balls – with controlled precision, when Tiger won the Masters by 12 strokes in 1997 it was obvious a whole new era in the game had begun. Yet this turned out to be just a forewarning – it was what he did in 2000 that left his peers gasping in wonder. At the US Open at Pebble Beach he won by 15 stokes and never three-putted. A month later at the Open at St. Andrews he again won comfortably and without finding a bunker on the Old Course. Els was a distant runner-up on each occasion. Woods went on to win the USPGA and then the Masters in 2001, becoming the first player ever to hold all four of the major trophies at the same time. Others, like Els, Vijay Singh, Phil Mickelson and David Duval had to grab what spoils they could, when they could. In women's golf, the game became increasingly global, with Laura Davies triumphing all round the world and Karrie Webb, Se Ri Pak, Lorena Ochoa and Yani Tseng emerging as stars. But for Tiger-like domination, there was no one to match Annika Sörenstam.

ERNIE ELS

Born October 17, 1969, Johannesburg, South Africa
US Open champion 1994 and '97; Open champion 2002

Ernie Els is such a familiar figure after two decades on tour that it is instructive to be reminded of his impact in the early 1990s. It was almost Greg Norman-like. He won the South African hat-trick of Open, PGA and Masters titles and Gary Player, whose mantle as his country's best player he inherited, said: 'When I first saw Ernie play golf I knew I was witnessing one of golf's next generation of superstars.' At six feet, three inches, he had a natural, graceful, fluid swing; such power, seemingly such little effort. 'The one thing that has stayed the same in my golf, ever since I was a boy, is my rhythm,' he said. European tour player Mark Roe said: 'The first time I played with him I was impressed immediately. It was his power, the sheer effortlessness of his swing.' Seve Ballesteros said he was a player from another planet. After Els won the US Open at the age of 24, Curtis Strange called him the 'next god of golf'.

He won again in 1997 at Congressional and then took the Open in 2002 in the first ever four-man playoff in a major. The previous Sunday night the first thing he had done on arriving at Muirfield was to view the scene at the 18th in the setting sun. 'If that does not inspire you,' he told his companion, 'nothing will.' Peter Dawson, the chief executive of the R&A, said: 'There is no side with Ernie, what you see is what you get. I enjoy his company immensely. He is a fine ambassador as our Open champion.'

They call him the 'Big Easy'. It matches his swing and his temperament. At least, most of the time. He is far too intense a competitor to live up to his laid-back image all the time. After two bogeys in the last three holes at the 1996 Open, a couple of unfortunates got both barrels in the locker room, followed by an apology. His golf has never dominated his life, even if a sailing trip in the Mediterranean in 2005 led to an anterior cruciate injury. His son Ben was diagnosed with autism, and raising awareness and money for autism charities is now more of a priority.

Els took the fight to Tiger Woods more than most but admitted he was embarrassed to finish 15 strokes behind at the 2000 US Open. He was runner-up again at the following Open. Els said: 'You can beat the field but it doesn't mean you're going to beat Tiger. If it wasn't for one guy, Mickelson might have two or three majors by now, David Duval might have won the Masters and who knows, I could have won four or five majors. This guy is a totally different talent than the world has ever seen. In a way I'm kind of glad I'm playing at this time and in another way I'm unhappy about it.'

VIJAY SINGH

Born February 22, 1963, Lautoka, Fiji
USPGA champion 1998 and 2004; Masters champion 2000

Like Ben Hogan, Vijay Singh, whose name means 'Victorious Lion', dug it out of the dirt. But this was no Texan dirt. This was the dirt of Fiji and Borneo, as well as the lush practice ranges of tournaments all over the world. Singh kept working and where did it get him? Three majors, most wins by an overseas player on the PGA Tour, most wins by anyone in their 40s on the American circuit, and the World Golf Hall of Fame. It is one of golf's most incredible journeys.

Singh, a Fijian of Indian-Hindu descent, was the son of an airport worker at Nadi, who was also captain of the golf club there. Getting to the course meant ducking down through the flowing drainage pipes under the runway, or sprinting across it. He read the golf magazines that came to the airport and, being tall and having a languid swing, he took particular notice of any swing sequences of Tom Weiskopf.

'I think the thing that has separated me is that I would do whatever it took,' Singh told *Golf Digest*. 'I did that from a young age, and it gave me the toughness. I didn't have any money, and I wasn't going to get any pocket money from my dad. He had six kids and in Fiji the taxes were about 50 per cent, and we never really lived comfortably. I understand how much pressure that put on him. My dad was a tough guy. He had to be. And to play golf, I had to be tough, too.'

ERNIE ELS

Vijay Singh

There was a rules incident in Indonesia when Singh was accused of altering his card. He said it was a misunderstanding with his marker. 'My marker was the son of a VIP in the Indonesian PGA, so to save some embarrassment they chose to get me.' Singh was not just disqualified but banned for two years. He took a club pro's job in the rain forests of Borneo. 'A loner, a fighter, a challenger who was banished from the world in which he wanted to live and play and then, like some tormented character in a Joseph Conrad novel, he lashed himself to the mast,' wrote sports journalist Art Spander. There was nothing to do but practise. Ardena, Singh's wife, recalled: 'God, when I look back at those times, I can't fathom how we managed to get from there to here. We didn't see people for weeks on end. It was totally desperate, and yet Vijay kept going, getting up early, practising, never losing sight of his dream. It has hardened his character.'

Eventually he escaped to the Safari Tour in Africa, then to Europe, where he was briefly a nightclub bouncer in Edinburgh, and then to the USA. He became a Masters champion and in 2004 topped the world money rankings. 'He is the only guy who got better, not just maintained his level, but got better in his 40s,' said Colin Montgomerie. Ernie Els said: 'I think people have a misconception of Vijay. Golf should be proud of him.'

JULI INKSTER

Born June 24, 1960, Santa Cruz, California
**US Women's Amateur champion 1980, '81 and '82;
Nabisco Dinah Shore champion 1984 and '89; du Maurier Classic
champion 1984; US Women's Open champion 1999 and 2002;
LPGA champion 1999 and 2000**

At the Solheim Cup in 2009 Juli Inkster became both the highest ever point scorer for America and the oldest player to play in the match. When she was announced as an assistant captain for the 2011 match in Ireland, it might have suggested that Inkster's golfing career was slowing down. Not a bit of it. At the age of 51,

JULI INKSTER

she qualified to play for America yet again, alongside team-mates who in some cases were no older than her own daughters. 'They call me Grandma,' she said. 'Kids on the tour say to me, "You're older than my mom." I think it's a compliment. With the beauty of this game, age is not really a factor.'

Playing golf may not be her whole life but it has been such a part of it that, despite last adding to her tally of 31 official victories in 2006, there has not yet been any thought of retirement. 'If you can still do it, do it,' has been her attitude. Her career has had three distinct phases. First she was a leading amateur who won the American national title three times in a row, becoming the first to do so since 1934. 'When I look back at it now I don't know how in the world I won three in a row because in match play you get somebody hot and you're out of there,' said Inkster. 'It's probably my best accomplishment as a golfer, either professional or amateur.' The first of her Amateur titles arrived in 1980 just weeks after marrying Brian Inkster, a club pro at Los Altos. This was where Juli Simpson had learnt the game, starting by parking the carts, moving on to working in the pro shop and then ever upwards.

Following her amateur career, she won her fifth start as a professional in 1983 and a new star was confirmed with two majors the next year and another in 1989.

Then came the third phase of her career as Hayley arrived in 1990 and Cori in 1994. Arguably her finest achievement was to raise her daughters as well as returning right to the top of her profession, two US Opens the crowning glory. 'Until I had kids, for almost my whole life my whole day was being Juli Inkster. It was about me. You have to be a little selfish.

'And then that all changed. There were a lot of times when I was running around with my head cut off, and in the mid-1990s my golf had to take a back seat.' At the opening ceremony for the 1998 Solheim Cup, her team-mates requested Inkster raise the American flag accompanied by her daughters. 'It was the moment I realised I could play golf and be a mother,' she said. Her best season followed in 1999.

Inkster added: 'My daughters know they are loved. My husband and I have made a stable home for them. They've grown up on golf courses. It wasn't easy but the kids never complained. They still don't. Every year I ask them what they think I should do and they say, "Keep playing".'

LAURA DAVIES

Born October 5, 1963, Coventry
Women's British Open champion 1986;
US Women's Open champion 1987; LPGA champion 1994 and '96;
du Maurier Classic champion 1996

Laura Davies has been playing almost as long as Juli Inkster, and has kept on winning. In 2010 she won five times and almost won the order of merit on the Ladies European Tour for an eighth time. She won in New Zealand and India, two rare places where she had not won before. Her 77th career win came in New Delhi in typically adventurous circumstances. Her clubs did not arrive on the same plane and only turned up on the morning of the first round. She dashed to the airport, got back moments before her tee-time and, without having played a practice round, she scored a 65. She has won every year since 1985, except in 2005. 'I love to play and I love to win,' she said.

But, as might be suggested by a golfer who has books to her name entitled *Carefree Golf* and *Naturally...*, it is Davies's uncomplicated approach to the game that is truly thrilling. She gives the ball an almighty thump. 'When Laura hits the ball, the earth shakes,' one player said. 'An inveterate gambler,' wrote Liz Kahn, 'she always takes chances and this penchant for taking risks, combined with her power, which allows her to attempt shots no other player would dare, creates an awesome sight on a golf course.' Her US Open win caused a sensation, as did Catherine Lacoste's. After a particularly risky blast to a blind par-five green in the playoff, JoAnne Carner asked: 'Why on earth would you have tried that?' Davies replied simply: 'No brains.'

Yet she learned by osmosis from watching the likes of Seve Ballesteros. When the Solheim Cup started in 1990, the US were massively stronger but two years later at Dalmahoy it was Davies

LAURA DAVIES

who led Europe to a huge upset. Her captain, Mickey Walker, said: 'Laura was simply willing the Solheim Cup victory. She has an incredible influence and power over the players, it's as though she is God. She doesn't realise it and they don't either. Laura is Laura, unique in every sense, as a talent, as a person, in whatever she has done.' In the mid-1990s she was the best woman player in the world and has always travelled the globe. In 1994 she topped the US money list and also won in Europe, Japan, Asia and Australia. She may well be the most influential woman golfer in growing the game around the world.

An interest in fast cars, gambling and sport were all part of growing up with her brother Tony. 'We were always competitive with each other. We had bets on everything we did. I wouldn't have a putt without a bet on it. Even at Trivial Pursuits we would play for a fiver. I'll always want to win because I'm so competitive. That will never change. The day I don't care, I'll give up.' She cares about gaining the required LPGA points for membership of the World Golf Hall of Fame but that misses the point: she should be in anyway for her global achievements.

SE RI PAK
Born September 28, 1977, Daejeon, South Korea
LPGA champion 1998, 2002 and '06;
US Women's Open champion 1998;
Women's British Open champion 2001

When it comes to influential victories in the US Women's Open by overseas players, those by Catherine Lacoste and Laura Davies are high on the list. Liselotte Neumann, of Sweden, won the year after Davies and led the way for Annika Sörenstam, a three-time champion. But in 1998 Se Ri Pak, a 20-year-old rookie, won at Blackwolf Run in Wisconsin. She was not only the youngest ever winner but also the first champion from South Korea. Pak had already won the LPGA Championship a few weeks earlier in

Se Ri Pak

a stunning wire-to-wire performance. At the Open, Pak hooked her drive into water on the last hole and had to wade in to play a remarkable recovery and get into a playoff with amateur Jenny Chuasiriporn, which Pak won at the 20th hole. Only Juli Inkster had previously won two majors in her rookie season and, coming from a country just becoming aware of golf, Pak's triumphs made her a star in her homeland. When she returned home at the end of the season she was awarded one of the country's highest honours, but such was the attention that she collapsed with exhaustion and spent four days in hospital.

Over the next decade the face of the women's game changed forever. An extraordinary explosion of South Korean players made their way to America, and many of them described being allowed to stay up in the middle of the night to watch Pak win in 1998. Birdie Kim, Inbee Park, Eun-Hee Ji and So Yeon Ryu all won the US Open, Grace Park the Nabisco Championship and Jeong Jang and Jiyai Shin the British Open. 'I've given them the confidence to come out here,' Pak said. 'I think of them like my sisters.' More South Koreans have won tour events but so far none has become a multiple major champion other than Pak, the youngest ever, at the age of 27, to be inducted into the World Golf Hall of Fame.

While until recently the development of male golfers in Korea was delayed by national service, young girls were exposed not just to the game but also to a relentless work ethic. Pak's father had Se Ri running up and down the staircases of their 15-storey apartment building at 5.30 in the morning to build leg strength, and sometimes took her to a cemetery in the middle of the night 'to develop courage and nerve,' he said. 'I wanted to teach her that to win in golf, she first had to win the battle within herself.'

Pak admitted to burn-out but recovered by taking control of her own life, which is perhaps why her most treasured honour is being voted by her fellow players as winner of the 2006 Heather Farr Award, which recognises a 'player who, through her hard work, dedication and love of the game of golf, has demonstrated determination, perseverance and spirit in fulfilling her goals'. 'Of all of my success for nine years, this award is the most important and biggest, maybe for the rest of my life,' she said.

Karrie Webb

KARRIE WEBB

Born December 21, 1974, Ayr, Queensland
Women's British Open 1995, '97 and 2002; du Maurier
Classic champion 1999; Kraft Nabisco champion 2000
and '06; US Women's Open champion 2000 and '01;
LPGA champion 2001

Just where does Karrie Webb come from? The easy answer is Ayr, in the remote north of Queensland around 1,000 miles from Brisbane. Where her golf comes from is another question. 'Sometimes I don't understand why I am sitting here,' Webb said, clutching the US Open trophy in 2000. 'I think I was given a gift to play golf and to be mentally strong. You know, I don't see a sports psychologist. I've somehow just known what to do.'

The first time she played in a competition she won the 'Encouragement Award' but was too young to realise that meant she had come last. 'Ayr is both hot and sweaty and a long way from anywhere,' wrote David Davies. 'The town has a population of 8,600 and most of them are involved either in the production of sugar cane or providing services for it. Webb's parents owned a toy and gift shop, right next door to the newsagents.' The son of the owners of the newsagents, Kelvin Haller, used to study all the golf magazines and, since the local golf club did not have a professional, Haller became Webb's coach. An accident led to Haller becoming a quadriplegic and confined to a wheelchair but he was still able to coach Webb, via email or on her annual visit back to Ayr.

Haller said: 'When I look back, I see her determination and her will to win and I think she is gifted in that way. I knew she was good but I didn't really have any idea. None of us did. It's a small town. When Karrie played in that first British Open, and – bang! – she won it, I guess we all started to catch on.' It was a victory that got everyone's attention, even if her first two British titles do not count as official LPGA majors. Her prime years were 1999 to 2002, when she won six majors, including five out of eight.

Peter Thomson rated Webb the best golfer in the world, man or woman, with a swing that was better than that of Tiger Woods. She had the ability to hit high iron shots that landed softly and with spin that was perfectly controlled. Meg Mallon, herself a double US Open champion, said: 'Sometimes when a player makes it look as easy as she does, it's hard to appreciate how good she is. She's one of the best ball-strikers ever on our tour.'

Webb was the youngest to earn a career grand slam and the first to earn a super slam when she won at Turnberry in 2002, when the British Open was designated a major after the demise of the du Maurier Classic. So swiftly did Webb earn the required number of points to enter the LPGA and World Golf Hall of Fame that she had to wait five years to complete the ten-season minimum. 'It seems like I've waited a long time for this, but looking back I can't believe how fast everything has gone and how much I've been able to accomplish.'

ANNIKA SÖRENSTAM

Born October 9, 1970, Stockholm, Sweden

US Women's Open champion 1995, '96 and 2006; Kraft Nabisco champion 2001, '02 and '05; LPGA champion 2003, '04 and '05; Women's British Open champion 2003

For the first half-decade of the new millennium the only player who could keep up with Tiger Woods's majors tally was Annika Sörenstam. Many were the bantering texts between them on the subject. When she won a third US Open in 2006, they both had ten, although Tiger would then pull ahead again. Although the Swede would soon lose her world No 1 tag to Lorena Ochoa, she was still a dominant figure in the game when she retired at the end of the 2008 season at the age of 38 to start a family. Or 'stepped away', as she put it, from competition. Now she has two children, an academy and a business under the ANNIKA brand.

At a time when world-class women players were emerging all around the globe, Sörenstam led the way. Back-to-back US Opens in the mid-1990s marked her arrival but it was in the noughties

when she really got going after coming to terms with life in the spotlight. She has always been shy. As a junior, Sörenstam was known to three-putt the last hole to avoid winning and having to speak publicly. When a coach decided that both the winner and the runner-up should make speeches, Sörenstam decided winning was better after all.

Pia Nilsson, the Swedish national coach, found a willing pupil in Sörenstam for her vision of scoring a 54, not limiting yourself, thinking you can birdie every hole. In 2001 at Moon Valley, Sörenstam got close. She was 12 under for 13 holes and scored the LPGA's first 59. By now a practice and fitness regime meant she had added power but she was always a meticulously accurate player: tidy house, tidy mind, tidy golfer.

In 2003 she became the first woman since Babe Zaharias (an exact opposite personality type) to play on the men's tour at Colonial. It created huge interest and the course, tight and not long, suited her game but she did not have the best putting week as she missed the cut by four strokes. The word went out that she could not putt under pressure, something that a score of 59, 72 LPGA wins (second only to Kathy Whitworth and Mickey Wright) and 89 worldwide victories somewhat disproves. She said: 'This is way over my head. I'm going back to my tour where I belong.' Two months later she won the British Open at Lytham, the one major on European soil and the one she wanted. She said then: 'I believe I have become a better player since playing at the Colonial. There were times today when I felt the pressure and then I thought it was not as bad as at the Colonial.'

A clinical, rather than emotional, golfer, she was nevertheless at her best in the Solheim Cup, especially helping Europe to victory at Barsebäck in Sweden in 2003. At the 2000 match at Loch Lomond, she gave a locker-room speech of such fire and passion that it was said to have been instrumental in beating the Americans.

TIGER WOODS

Born December 30, 1975, Cypress, California
US Amateur champion 1994, '95 and '96;
Masters champion 1997, 2001, '02 and '05;
USPGA champion 1999, 2000, '06 and '07;
US Open champion 2000, '02 and '08;
Open champion 2000, '05 and '06

When Tiger Woods emerged as the best golfer of his generation, he played golf with an intensity, relentlessness and
determination to win rarely seen in combination with such calmness, clear thinking and clinical application to the game. Arnold
Palmer said: 'Tiger's biggest strength is that he can play Jack
Nicklaus's style, waiting for his chances, and he can play in my
style, attacking all the time. That's some combination.' Nicklaus
said: 'When he gets ahead, I think he is superior to me. I never
spread-eagled the field.'

Three successive US Juniors and three successive US Amateurs
were merely historical footnotes before he won his first major as
a professional, the 1997 Masters, by 12 strokes. It changed golf,
although the effect on the leading players' bank balances may have
been greater than his influence on the racial profile of the game. But
it was the first globally viewed golfing miracle. The next was even
more sublime. In the summer of 2000 he played the best golf anyone
has ever played. He won the US Open by 15 strokes and the Open
Championship by eight. He never three-putted at Pebble Beach and
he never visited a bunker on the Old Course. At Pebble he was 12
under, then a record score, but no one else was better than three
over. One of the runners-up, Ernie Els, said: 'He is a phenomenon,
but anything I say is an understatement. We're not playing in the
same ballpark right now.'

Woods won the USPGA and then the 2001 Masters, not the first-
ever calendar-year grand slam but he said: 'I've got all four trophies
sitting on my coffee table.' Other standout performances were the
2006 Open, two months after the death of his father, with a breath-
taking display of controlled mid- and long-iron shots on a baked

TIGER WOODS

Hoylake, and the incredible 2008 US Open at Torrey Pines with a broken leg and against doctors' orders.

Since then, his attempt to break Nicklaus's record of 18 professional major titles has stalled at 14. Injury has meant four operations on his left knee and another lengthy period out of action in 2011. There was also scandal and divorce, all unfolding after a car crash outside his home on the night after Thanksgiving 2009, amid reports he had a mistress – it soon turned out he had many more besides.

Perhaps his greatest achievement is yet to come as he tries to rehabilitate his body, his game and his reputation. Somewhere along the way, the thing that got lost was his passion for the game itself. It was obvious at first, with all those extravagant fist-pumps after a chip-in or a monster putt holed. However, a major problem was that his style and personality did not translate to the team environment of the Ryder Cup. He was always a man apart. It was different for him, he thought, and we were instructed to believe this. It was once said 'his meanness, his pettiness, his cheapness' were vital to the package of this supreme champion. Nothing unique in that. But what a rise, what a fall, what next?

PHIL MICKELSON

Born June 16, 1970, San Diego, California
US Amateur champion 1990; Masters champion 2004, '06 and '10; USPGA champion 2005

If Tiger Woods barely blinked between being US Amateur champion and winning his first professional major, it was a 14-year wait for Phil Mickelson. He had long been the new Bear apparent but as his near-misses mounted up, so Tiger was almost haunting him with major after major, eight of them, often at Lefty's expense, before Mickelson won the Masters in 2004. Three years earlier, at the USPGA after losing to David Toms, Mickelson had despaired: 'The frustration is not because I'm trying to win a major. I'm trying to win a bunch of them.' Once Woods arrived, it was a currency that appreciated rapidly. Mickelson beat Ernie Els, another to suffer at Tiger's hands, in a thrilling contest at Augusta and then did indeed go on to collect a 'bunch of them'.

He had said: 'I don't feel pressed for time. Hogan only started winning majors at the age of 34. I just want to give myself the best chance at each one.' Mickelson was 33 when he claimed his first green jacket. Whether he always gave himself the best chance of winning a major is debatable. Perhaps no one since Seve Ballesteros drove the ball so poorly and had such a magical short game. There was never any question about his natural talent – learning the game by standing next to his father and producing a mirror image, playing on a par-three course from the age of six, winning as an amateur on the PGA Tour – but doubts remained as to whether he could temper his natural aggression long enough to avoid disaster. Yes, he could, it turned out, but not at a US Open, where he has been a runner-up five times. He should have won at Winged Foot in 2006, but then so should Colin Montgomerie. Monty lost it with his second shot, Mickelson, as ever, with a drive that was last seen enjoying corporate hospitality.

In 2007, Mickelson employed Butch Harmon as his coach. Harmon turned first Greg Norman and then, for that spell at the turn of the millennium, Woods into the longest, straightest drivers in the game. It has not quite worked with Mickelson but it is an intriguing relationship, as Lefty has with his short game specialist, Dave Pelz, a former NASA scientist. Harmon said: 'He is even more talented than I thought and I knew he was exceptionally talented going into this.'

There is no sound on earth quite as loud as a New York gallery's support for Mickelson. The goofy smile might have been grating for British viewers earlier in his career but there is genuine love for Mickelson amongst American golf fans, while even at the height of his powers there was only respect for Woods. There was no more heart-warming sight than Mickelson being embraced at the 18th green at the 2010 Masters by his wife Amy, who a year earlier was diagnosed with breast cancer, as had Mickelson's mother almost simultaneously. He has always been a family man first, golfer second.

Phil Mickelson

David Duval

DAVID DUVAL
Born November 9, 1971, Jacksonville, Florida
Open champion 2001

D avid Duval removed his cap and his wraparound sunglasses, collected the claret jug and smiled, and gave a fine winner's speech at the 2001 Open. Everything had changed. The real David Duval had stepped forward, we thought. We were wrong, for Duval was only just about to discover his real self. What we knew up until then was a fine golfer who had shot a 59 to win a tournament, won the 1999 Players Championship and dethroned Tiger Woods as the best player in the world. He had come so close to winning a number of majors.

Other facts included the death of his brother Brent from aplastic anaemia, that the child David had donated bone marrow and blamed himself for Brent's death, and that his parents had divorced amid the grief. He was said to be a 'boy who loved to golf alone in a fog. It was as if the sky was colluding with him, lowering a grey curtain between him and the world.' He was a reader, too thoughtful to give pat press answers. He was overweight, then a fitness freak. He could not win, with 11 top-threes before his first victory; then could not stop winning, 11 times in two years.

He had finally won his major. But of that night, John Hawkins wrote: 'What struck me was the utter lack of joy exhibited by anyone in the travelling party, particularly the latest owner of the claret jug. You would have sworn Duval finished tied for 35th.' One more win followed in Japan later in the year but his game was already suffering from repeated back, neck and wrist injuries. He also experienced what he called an 'existential moment'. 'When you work so hard,' he recalled, 'and have had so many near misses and then win, and you didn't play that well, it's like, "Are you kidding? Are you really gonna do this to me?" It's not like I played bad, but of the tournaments I won, that's the one I played the worst in.'

A long-term relationship ended, his game and ambitions in tatters. He said: 'When you're a successful athlete in our society, not only are you not allowed to play poorly, you're not really allowed to be human. I'm 32 years old. You start seeking things in your life, putting together the missing pieces. Just like anybody does.'

Duval met a woman in Denver, moved there, got married, became a stepfather of three and then a father of two more. His golf has yet to find the old consistency yet he finds far more pleasure in it. He almost won the US Open in 2009, ranked 882nd in the world. 'If it wasn't for Susie and these kids, I would have stopped playing golf a few years ago. They taught me what I am is not what I do; they showed me I don't have to be golf. But golf is still so ingrained in my psyche, it takes a conscious effort for me to separate "David" from "golf".'

RETIEF GOOSEN

Born February 3, 1969, Pietersburg, South Africa
US Open champion 2001 and '04

Retief Goosen was the man to stop Tiger Woods's winning streak in 2001. Tiger held all four majors but had to give back the US Open without contending. The finish was ugly. Goosen, Mark Brooks and Stewart Cink all three-putted the last green. Goosen missed from two feet for the title. Johnny Miller on television called it 'the worst three-putt in the history of golf'. British golf writer David Davies wrote: 'It was possibly the most calamitous loss of nerve ever seen in a major championship. Never was a shorter, easier putt for a major title missed.' But, thanks to his perseverance and the help of a sports psychologist, Jos Vanstiphout, Goosen came back the next day to beat Brooks, the 1996 USPGA champion, in an 18-hole playoff.

His putting could occasionally be wayward but not at Shinnecock Hills in 2004. The greens were so firm and fast they were almost unplayable but Goosen produced one of the greatest displays ever seen on the greens. He single-putted 12 times in the final round to beat Phil Mickelson, who had the whole of New York supporting him. Goosen joined Ernie Els as a double champion. He two-putted at the last and tipped his cap. 'It was a small relief. It was more

we've done it this time on a Sunday and don't have to come back on Monday. I'm not really somebody that jumps up and down, as we know, but on the inside I was just, like, so happy.'

Succeeding at US Open golf has always required a special temperament. Goosen has it but the way he got it is not something to try at home. Playing with friends at Pietersburg a few days before his 16th birthday, the group was caught by a sudden thunderstorm. A lightning bolt hit a nearby tree with such ferocity that Goosen was knocked unconscious, his clothes were burnt away and his rubber shoes melted. He only remembers waking up in hospital 'feeling sore and covered in skin burns. There is nothing left of it now but at the time I was a bit of a mess.' There were related health issues for a time and his mother, Annie, believes the accident left him more introverted than he had been before. He remains softly spoken and accident prone, once crashing while skiing in Switzerland but only discovering some weeks later that his arm was broken.

Goosen has an alternative explanation for keeping his golfing temperament under control. 'I haven't always been calm on the course. I've been known to lose it and break the odd club. In fact, just before I turned pro I remember breaking three clubs in nine holes. But it got expensive when my dad said I had to pay for the new shafts.' He also credits his English wife Tracy with helping him to conquer his negative thoughts, while he described the wedding in 2001 as one of the most nerve-racking moments of his life. The US Open a couple of months later may not have felt such an ordeal after all.

SERGIO GARCIA

Born January 9, 1980, Castellón, Spain
Amateur champion 1998

At the time of writing (2011), there has occasionally been the hint of the odd smile returning to the face of Sergio Garcia. This is very good news indeed. The sullen, and at times surly, Sergio is not how he should be remembered. No, it was his infectious enthusiasm

Sergio Garcia

that was so attractive. The image remains of the 19-year-old rookie chasing Tiger Woods home at the 1999 USPGA, literally so after a shot from behind a tree at Medinah's 16th, skipping up the fairway and cresting the brow of a hill to see the end result. He stormed into the thick of several Ryder Cups with seemingly endless energy. Over the last two years, that energy has seeped away. Was it the major near misses, the putts refusing to drop, the ending of a relationship with Greg Norman's daughter, Morgan-Leigh?

The son of a professional, Garcia has never been orthodox. There is the loop at the top of the backswing, the waggling and re-gripping. But he hits the ball as purely as anyone ever has done. At Carnoustie in 2007, he led for three days but then the putts dried up. He missed chances on the 72nd and the 76th holes that seemed certain to drop but Padraig Harrington took the title. 'It seems I have no room for error. I am playing against more than just the field,' Garcia said darkly. A year later he lost the USPGA in another close contest with the Irishman. 'He's an incredible talent and probably the best ball-striker in the game,' Harrington said. 'He's young and he's going to win a major, he's going to win majors. It's going to happen. The more he believes that the quicker it will happen.'

By the end of 2008 he was the Players champion and the world number two. Two years later he was smashing up the face of a bunker – previously having spat into the cup of a hole after three-putting among other misdemeanours – and announced he was taking a two-month break. 'I need to miss the game a bit,' he said. He turned up as a vice-captain at the Ryder Cup but was never in with a chance of playing.

Spain, Europe and golf's next big thing was nowhere. He said: 'For almost as long as I can remember, everyone's been saying, "When are you going to win a major?" The truth is that whatever people might think, it's not something that has ever kept me awake at night.' He was a good kid, El Niño, if prone to over-exuberance, arrogance even. 'Seve Ballesteros has more than once publicly rued the loss of his childhood years to golf, and Sergio, who started playing in professional events at 14 years of age, has clearly been tangling with similar emotions,' wrote Lewine Mair. Now in his early 30s he is looking for more from life. As much a family man as his friend Rafa Nadal, Garcia is at heart a good guy. His golf may just need patience.

PADRAIG HARRINGTON
Born August 31, 1971, Dublin, Ireland
Open champion 2007 and '08; USPGA champion 2008

Padraig Harrington has one of the most original minds in golf. No one, perhaps not even himself, is sure what he is going to come up with next. Here is a golfer who did all his accountancy exams, seemed to be heading for a comfortable if unspectacular golfing career, then suddenly won three major championships, then decided to change his swing again. He once said to the press: 'It is your job to have expectations of me. It is my job not to let that affect the expectations I have of myself.'

His father, who died in 2005, was a police officer in the Gardaí and helped build a course at Stackstown, south of Dublin. The young Harrington, whose father, uncle and two brothers were all single-figure handicappers, spent much of his youth playing there. 'I would have settled for being a journeyman when I turned professional but I started so well that I always had the focus to improve and see how good I could become,' he said.

He worked and worked, often for days on end, with Bob Torrance, the coach and father of Sam, at Largs. He won occasionally, came second far more often (29 times and counting) but then in 2007 he won the Irish Open, his 'fifth major'. His first Open win at Carnoustie followed, amid the mayhem of twice going in the Barry Burn at the 18th for a double bogey but still beating Sergio Garcia in the playoff. 'I proved before that I am capable of making things difficult for myself,' he said. His obsession with practising included smashing drivers into a beanbag late at night even after winning the Irish PGA in 2008. He injured his wrist and his defence of the claret jug, just days away, was in doubt.

Padraig Harrington

He hardly practised at Birkdale but prevailed brilliantly on the Sunday. A month later he became the first European who was not a naturalised American to win the USPGA, again beating Garcia at Oakland Hills.

At Carnoustie Harrington became only the second Irishman to win the Open, after Fred Daly 60 years earlier, and the first European to win a major in the new century. He was the first of a new wave of European stars to break through and those that have followed have attributed their success to his. 'Michael Campbell winning the US Open was a big help to me because I knew him and knew his game. It was easier to visualise myself winning a major after he did,' Harrington explained. 'Other major champions like Els, Goosen and Woods, I would have put on a pedestal. They were unbeliev-able players and it felt like they never hit a bad shot. It was always, if you play your best, you *might* beat Tiger. But the guys that know me, have played with me, know my game, know I hit good shots, I hit bad shots, I work hard, they *know* they can beat me. And if they can beat me, they can win a major, too.'

LORENA OCHOA

Born November 15, 1981, Guadalajara, Mexico
**Women's British Open champion 2007;
Kraft Nabisco champion 2008**

Lorena Ochoa was not quite as young as Catherine Lacoste when she retired from golf. In fact she was the same age as Bobby Jones, 28, but the effect was the same as with the Frenchwoman – a bright star had shone luminously and was then gone. For three years Ochoa was the best woman golfer on the planet, seamlessly following on from Annika Sörenstam. But then in April 2010, she suddenly announced she was retiring from the sport. She had mar-ried a Mexican airline executive the year before and at the start of the new season found her motivation lacking. She had dreamed of retiring as the world No 1 and that wish was fulfilled. She said: 'I want to dedicate to my family the time I have taken from them all these years.'

Ochoa was Mexico's first golfing star, learning the game as she grew up in Guadalajara from local professional Rafael Alarcon, who played for Mexico in the old Dunhill Cup. Ochoa was successful on the American college circuit and soon won on the LPGA tour. In 2006 the victories started mounting up and the following year she dethroned Sörenstam. Clearly the outstanding player in the game, only one thing had eluded her – a major. It was a talking point when she arrived at St. Andrews for the first professional major championship for women on the Old Course. 'I think my family and the media worry more than me,' Ochoa said. She added: 'Here we are, we need to stand on the first tee with a big smile, appreciate it and enjoy every step and every moment.' Her victory was never in doubt, her triumphant parade at the 18th matching anything from Tiger Woods and the men.

'This was my time,' she said. 'It's a blessing the whole week. I wanted to win the tournament so badly and I worked so hard. I had the picture in my mind of me lifting the trophy but I always thought very clearly. I just said to myself, "I am ready". It has been a long wait for a major but now I can see it was for a reason. This is the most special tournament I've ever played.' Ochoa won the next major, the Kraft Nabisco in 2008, but they are the only two among her 27 victories in six years.

In almost two-thirds of her tournaments she finished in the top ten but what was memorable was that she was a happy golfer. She started every press interview with a beaming smile and the words: 'Hello, everyone.' It should not be noteworthy but somehow it is. She always visited the staff behind the scenes at tournaments, since many were of Mexican descent. Many a breakfast she had in the greenkeepers' hut. 'She did more than regularly win golf tournaments,' said Mike Whan, the LPGA commissioner. 'She fully embraced her role as global ambassador for the sport, raising its stature not only in her beloved home country but around the world.'

YANI TSENG

Born January 23, 1989, Guishan, Taiwan
**LPGA champion 2008 and '11; Kraft Nabisco champion 2010;
Women's British Open champion 2010 and '11**

After the sudden retirement of Lorena Ochoa, a number of players became the world number one according to the rankings, but sooner than anyone had imagined another player came along to dominate women's golf. At the age of 22 Yani Tseng was the youngest ever player, male or female, to win five major championships. Only Young Tom Morris had been younger in winning four majors, a mark Tseng reached in 2011 at the LPGA Championship where her margin of victory was ten strokes. A month later she successfully defended her title at the Ricoh Women's British Open at Carnoustie. It was the first time the women's tournament had been competed for on the famous links where Cotton, Hogan, Player and Watson were also champions. 'There are so many great players making history on this course,' she said. 'It is my honour to be a part of it.'

Having won four of the last eight majors, Tseng's dominance was already taking on historical proportions and there is much speculation about what she may ultimately achieve. 'At this rate, with her talent level, and after a couple more major wins, the conversation will shift to Patty Berg and her record 15 LPGA majors,' wrote Ron Sirak in *Golf World*. 'Hey, if Yani can knock Young Tom out of the record book, why not Old Patty?'

'You look at Yani and you never think there will be another Mickey Wright or another Annika Sörenstam or Lorena and all of a sudden Yani comes along,' said Juli Inkster. 'Yani has Lorena's power, she can bomb the ball. She's got a lot of passion for the game. She wants to be the best. She wants to get better. So she could be here for a while. If she stays healthy, she could probably break a lot of Annika's records.'

Sörenstam won ten majors but did not gain her fifth until the age of 32. Always Tseng's idol, the Swede became a mentor to the Taiwanese player after Tseng bought Sörenstam's old house at Lake

Lorena Ochoa

YANI TSENG

Nona in Orlando at the start of 2010. The house featured a huge trophy case. 'I looked at the empty case and I know I have to work hard to fill it up with trophies,' Tseng said. She took a bottle of wine and, admitting to being tongue-tied, went round the corner to Sörenstam's new abode. 'She picked my brains on becoming the best player,' Sörenstam said. 'She wants to learn but already her mental capacity may be as strong as her long game.'

A fine pool player – she says it helps with her putting – Tseng is the daughter of a club professional father and a caddie mother, and learned the game aged six by mimicking her parents' swings. Her father taught her to hit the ball hard. Harnessing that power came later but her fitness adviser, Andrea Doddato, says she has 'never seen a female athlete with so much upper-body explosive power'. Her medicine ball throws can leave the catcher reeling, just like her opponents on the course.

LEE WESTWOOD

Born April 24, 1973, Worksop, Nottinghamshire

There was a time when Lee Westwood could not stop winning. From 1996 to 2000 the son of a maths teacher from Worksop won 14 times in Europe and eight times worldwide, including the States. In 2000 he dethroned Colin Montgomerie as the European number one. 'I've always been able to keep my cool and win tournaments when I've got into contention,' he said. 'That's more about what's in your stomach and your heart really, rather than about technique.'

But then came a slump so severe he fell from fourth in the world to 266th. Suddenly, his game was gone and he won only twice (both within weeks) in seven years. He got out of the slump only after taking a 'ruthless and honest' look at himself and his career. He began a disciplined fitness programme – Gary Player had said years before that he needed to, and now he did. Westwood also returned to his coach Peter Cowen.

Consistency was now the hallmark of Westwood's game, and in 2009 he became the European number one for the second time. Wins were not plentiful but he was always the player to beat. If anything, his long game was so good that his putting suffered by comparison. There was an inevitability about Westwood being the man who would overtake Tiger Woods as the world number one, and it occurred in late October 2010. Andrew 'Chubby' Chandler, his manager, pointed to a few weeks earlier, saying: 'You only had to look at the Ryder Cup, where he walked around Celtic Manor like he owned the place: "I am Lee Westwood and I am the best player here."'

In seven Ryder Cups, Westwood has missed only one session of play and proved a vital part of Europe's recent successes, particularly when partnering his friend Darren Clarke in the 2006 match at the K Club. Yet, Clarke and other members of the International Sports Management stable such as Rory McIlroy, have won majors but Westwood ended 2011 with his account still blank. In a run of 12 majors, he was third four times and second twice, but Phil Mickelson brilliantly snatched away the 2010 Masters and a three-putt on the last green denied him a chance of a playoff for the 2009 Open. Turnberry may be his biggest regret. 'I came very close to winning what for me is the biggest tournament, the most important tournament in the world,' he said.

Married to Ryder Cup colleague Andrew Coltart's sister, Laurae, with two children, Westwood has never been tempted to leave his home town. A wry humour and self-deprecation have made him a Twitter hit. When he got a call to say he was the world number one he was shopping for 'a pair of rubber gloves and mashed potatoes'. A week later an air stewardess complimented his tan and asked what he had been up to. 'Playing a bit of golf,' he said. 'Are you any good?' she asked. 'Yes,' he replied, 'I'm the best in the world.'

DARREN CLARKE
Born August 14, 1968, Dungannon, Northern Ireland
Open champion 2011

It was while helping to celebrate Rory McIlroy's US Open victory that Darren Clarke was told to 'pull my finger out'. Clarke said he was not jealous, just very proud of McIlroy, whom he has mentored for a decade, and Graeme McDowell, the 2010 US Open champion. Yet within weeks of McIlroy's triumph, Clarke had his own, lifting the claret jug at Sandwich.

There was never any doubt about Clarke's talent, only about how much of his potential would be fulfilled. A handshake with Andrew 'Chubby' Chandler, in a manner reminiscent of Arnold Palmer and Mark McCormack, led to Chandler setting up a management company to look after Clarke when he turned professional. Soon the wins came. He almost shot Europe's first 59, he beat Tiger Woods head-to-head in the final of the 2000 WGC Accenture Matchplay and he became the first player other than Tiger to win two World Golf Championships. He spent as he earned, enjoying the luxuries of fast cars and fine cigars.

But in 2006 his wife Heather died from breast cancer. In emotional scenes at the Ryder Cup at the K Club, Clarke played brilliantly. Of his opening tee shot, which went right down the middle, he said: 'Pressure shots come no bigger. There will never be a harder shot or hole for me. If I am ever lucky enough to have a chance of winning a major or a really big title again, it won't compare.'

It took five years for Clarke to have a chance to prove it. In the meantime he had moved his sons, Tyrone and Conor, back to Northern Ireland, become engaged and spent the previous winter playing Royal Portrush with friends. Out in all weathers, they would have a 'couple of pints before and several more after'. Playing superb links golf, tacking his away around Royal St. George's in often blustery weather, Clarke achieved his dream. Helped by not one, but two, sports psychologists, Clarke remained calm as never before.

He said: 'In terms of what's going through my heart, there's obviously somebody who is watching down from up above there and I

DARREN CLARKE

know she would be very proud of me. She'd probably be saying "told you so". But I think she'd be more proud of my two boys and them at home watching more than anything else. It's been a long journey.'

At the age of 42, he admitted appreciating the victory more than he might have done earlier in his career and that there would be no personal treats this time. 'I've been there and done that all before, haven't I?' he said. 'To get my name on this thing,' he added, gesturing at the claret jug, 'and being able to show it to my boys, means more than anything.' Just before the Open, Clarke's boys were looking at Fred Daly's Open medal from 1947 in the Portrush clubhouse. 'Your dad hasn't got his hands on one of them, yet,' they were told by an assistant professional. He has now, and it rests beside that of Daly.

RORY MCILROY

Born May 4, 1989, Holywood, County Down
US Open champion 2011

Snap judgements cannot always be trusted, but all those experts who took one look at Rory McIlroy swinging a club and predicted he would win a major championship were proved right at the 2011 US Open.

McIlroy's swing is the talk of the practice range. 'It is one of the most graceful swings,' said Padraig Harrington. 'It is very co-ordinated. The more coordinated a swing, the slower it looks yet Rory manages to get so much clubhead speed. It's the sound of the strike. He hits the ball beautifully.' Colin Montgomerie added: 'He has a natural ability. Seve looked empty without a golf club in his hands. Ernie looks better with a golf club in his hands. Rory is the same now. Real, natural, God-given talent.' 'He's like a BMW,' said Graeme McDowell, 'the ultimate driving machine.'

McIlroy's achievements had been mounting up: a 61 in competition at Royal Portrush as a teenager; the silver medal as leading amateur at the 2007 Open; only two events required for him to earn a European Tour card; almost the youngest player since Seve

Rory McIlroy

Ballesteros to win the European order of merit in 2009, but for Lee Westwood; a closing 62 for his first win in the States in 2010; and a Ryder Cup debut the same year, where he admitted his earlier suggestion that the match was 'only an exhibition' had been wide of the mark.

At the Masters in 2011, McIlroy led for 63 holes and then imploded on the back nine at Augusta. Suddenly, he went from looking like the next golfing great to a heart-broken kid. Many worried if he possessed the killer instinct. McIlroy dismissed it as a one-off, worked on his putting and went to Congressional with a renewed strut. Four days later he had won by eight strokes with a record score and never looked like losing. The American gallery roared their approval. Jack Nicklaus liked his 'moxie', while Harrington predicted McIlroy would be the player to challenge Nicklaus's 18 majors. McIlroy's reply was a modest 'Paddy, Paddy, Paddy,' and a shake of the head.

Everyone was wowed. John Huggan wrote in *Scotland on Sunday*: 'Like all true greats, McIlroy has an innate ability to make an endlessly complicated and difficult game appear simple. With a club in his hands, he is Torvill and Dean on the ice, he is Frank Sinatra at the microphone and he is Lionel Messi with a ball at his feet. He has the potential to raise a mere sport to art form.'

Whatever he does or does not achieve in the future, he produced one of the great performances at Congressional. Afterwards, he showed he still has more to learn. Darren Clarke could give him some tips about coping with bad weather at an Open, while he admitted the shot against a tree root that injured his right wrist at the 2011 USPGA was foolhardy. But, as with Palmer, Seve and Tiger, whatever he is up to, it is hard to take your eyes off him.

CONCLUSION

Having selected our 100 greatest ever golfers, inevitably the next question is which one is the greatest of them all? Before we consider that, it is worth reflecting that no golfer, however great, is perfect. Lee Trevino said: 'God never gives it all to one person – except maybe Jack Nicklaus.' But perhaps even Nicklaus did not have it all. Others had better short games and, occasionally, he could have been more aggressive. What about Bobby Jones? As a young man he was hot-headed enough to quit during the third round of the 1921 Open at St. Andrews, although he played out the rest of that round and the next as a marker. Jones scaled the greatest of heights but then retired, whereas others had the gift of longevity.

But if we could pick our perfect golfer, what would he or she look like? Which player was the best driver, the best with the irons, had the best short game, or was deadliest on the greens? Let's start with the swing. Harry Vardon must be the man to start with for an upright swing, and then Byron Nelson for such a repeating motion. Bobby Jones must be in there, his 'drowsy grace' belying the power that he rarely unleashed but with which he occasionally surprised Sam Snead, blowing it past Sam when a par five allowed. Snead, of course, for his flexibility and longevity; Christy O'Connor Snr for natural fluidity; the effortlessness of Ernie Els, the 'Big Easy'; the sweet smoothness of wee Ian Woosnam; the efficiency of Ben Hogan's pared-down swing. Joyce Wethered, with her 'perfect equilibrium', had the most supreme balance, while Tony Jacklin won the

US Open concentrating solely on his tempo. Mickey Wright, whose swing was described as a combination of Jones's grace and Hogan's efficiency, hit the ball with such authority and arguably came closest to capturing it all.

Vardon, rarely seen in the rough, and Nelson were two of the straightest players ever; Hale Irwin, Colin Montgomerie and Annika Sörenstam some of their modern equivalents. Moe Norman was hardly orthodox, but Hogan told him to keep hitting the 'accidents' that went dead straight. When it comes to driving, however, few could beat Jack Nicklaus. The Bear himself said Hogan's exhibition of driving at the 1960 US Open was the best he had seen, and at Carnoustie in the 1953 Open they said Hogan's drives at the dangerous sixth (out of bounds on the left, bunkers centre and right) finished in the same divot every time. Rory McIlroy might be the ultimate driving machine today but what Nicklaus did with the equipment of his day was remarkable. 'With a wooden driver it was difficult to be long but he had the power to be long and was also accurate,' said Ken Brown. 'People hit it as hard as him but they didn't have his control.'

For a period in the early 1990s, Greg Norman was certainly the longest-straightest driver in the world and it helped him win the Open in 1993. At the time he was coached by Butch Harmon, who did a similar trick with Tiger Woods, who was a fine driver when he played with such control around the turn of the millennium. But later, when Tiger more often lashed at the ball, there were times when he could not keep it on the planet. In the women's game, the first to really develop huge power was the magnificent Babe Zaharias, whose athleticism and sheer *joie de vivre* sent the ball distances never seen before.

Gene Sarazen's albatross (double eagle) in the 1935 Masters qualifies him for recognition with fairway woods, and in this respect you could also mention Nelson and Gary Player. For a driver off the fairway, however, Henry Cotton amazed Henry Longhurst and friends. He could also knock over a shooting stick from 20 paces with a one-iron. Lee Trevino might have said not even God could hit a one-iron but Sandy Lyle certainly could. Snead must also get a mention, although once again Nicklaus probably takes the accolade. He singled out three one-iron shots in particular during his career, one of them the shot at the 17th hole at Pebble Beach which won him the 1972 US Open. Catherine Lacoste was a firecracker of a golfer who smacked a one-iron unlike any woman before her.

John Ball first showed what could be achieved with accurate approach play with iron clubs. Not for him merely finding a remote part of the green. Observers of Tommy Armour marvelled at his ball-striking with the irons, while Nelson, again, must be mentioned for his approach play. But you could do worse than look to three Europeans who won the Masters: Sir Nick Faldo, Bernhard Langer and José María Olazábal. Few courses demand such a high degree of precision as Augusta National, and that trio were rarely hitting their approach shots with anything as short as a wedge. From the 100-yard range, however, no one did it better than Walter Hagen.

Getting up-and-down from greenside bunkers was virtually impossible until Sarazen invented the sand wedge, but it was Player who made it into an art form. Norman Von Nida was better out of sand than he was on the greens, and at times he aimed for the bunkers. At least then he might hole one or simply have a tap-in. Ernie Els has been the best of the modern players. When it comes to chipping, Phil Mickelson and Woods must be up there, but no one was better than Seve Ballesteros. From the moment he threaded a running chip between the bunkers at Birkdale in the 1976 Open, we knew a unique talent had arrived. He had the skill to read the terrain, the imagination to 'see' a shot, the technique to execute it and, above all, the self-belief to pull off the outrageous. Olazábal learned by osmosis from his friend and partner.

Putting, of course, is the game within a game. Willie Park Snr, the first Open champion, was a fine putter and used the same club as he did for driving huge distances. His son was an even better putter and said something that Ben Crenshaw took on board – that a man who could putt was a match for anyone. Crenshaw died putts into the hole beautifully, while Raymond Floyd stared them in. Bobby Locke seemed to be tipping his hat to the crowd when a 50-footer was only halfway to the hole. Billy Casper had great hands but his wristy action was the opposite of Bob Charles's more pendulum-like motion. John Daly must get a shout for his lag-putting, particularly on the vast greens of St. Andrews, while Marlene Stewart Streit broke the spirit of many opponents by failing to miss, as had Walter Travis many years earlier, and Kathy Whitworth may be one of the greatest holer-outers ever. But when it comes to pressure putts, who can look beyond the triumvirate of Jones, Nicklaus and Woods? If one was better than the other two, well, answers on a postcard.

There are a few other factors to take into account, such as course management. Here, you would want Peter Thomson on board, as well as Nicklaus. Both had the priceless ability to think calmly under pressure, but others to look at would be Vardon, Jones, Hogan, Player and Woods (when not smashing his driver). But on the other hand, we want to be thrilled as well. Might there be a place for the 'divine fury' of James Braid or the 'controlled abandon' of Joe Carr? You would want the sheer whatever-will-happen-next unpredictability of Arnold Palmer, Ballesteros and Laura Davies – it would be risky and would not involve going backwards. The scrambling skills of Tom Watson and Mickelson could be added to the mix, with Watson adding the perseverance to get through any weather, as he has shown at many Opens, not least Sandwich in 2011.

When it comes to competitive longevity in the game, Watson is also on the list, along with John Ball, Snead, Julius Boros, Roberto de Vicenzo and Juli Inkster – plus Nicklaus, of course, for winning majors over almost a quarter of a century. Personality – a combination of Arnie and Seve, Jimmy Demaret and Nancy Lopez (hint to modern players: they all smiled), with both the modesty of Jones and the *braggadocio* of Hagen, is not too much to ask, is it? Oh, and this mythical creature would get on with it. Maybe not quite at the gallop of George Duncan but definitely without the dawdle introduced by Armour, Locke, Nicklaus and seemingly everyone nowadays.

One thing our perfect golfer should not be is *too* perfect. But then 'golf is not a game of perfect', as sports psychologist Bob Rotella tells us. Peter Dobereiner worried that if players worked so hard that they approached perfection, then 'pro golf would become unwatchable and would die.' He added: 'Nobody loves a machine and nobody would want to take up a game that a machine can play better than a human.'

People have always worried about improving standards in golf. Even in 1899, when Horace Hutchinson was trying to grapple with the task of assessing the relative merits of Young Tom Morris, of yesteryear, with the then titan, Harry Vardon, he noted how different the game had become. 'Scores are recorded now that were never dreamt of five-and-twenty years ago; courses are undoubtedly kept in much better condition nowadays, the horse mower was an unknown luxury to the ancients,' Hutchinson wrote. 'Again, clubs have improved and players have the advantage of many years experience in connection with the manufacture of balls.'

Perhaps any change, at any time, feels fundamental, but the recent shift so heavily in favour of power, thanks to highly engineered clubs and balls and better athleticism among the performers, certainly seems to be a pivotal time for the game. 'The modern equipment has made it a power game,' said Denis Pugh, a respected coach. 'If you ask what three skills you need, it would be power, power and power. Then you need to be able to chip and putt, but if you can putt, the chipping is not so important. If you can hit the ball 350 yards off the tee, you don't miss many greens with a wedge. So chipping becomes less of a skill you require and if you can putt, or rather if you don't miss putts, you tend to see a low score going on the card.'

As well as better courses and equipment, coaching – there are kids all over the globe now with what David Leadbetter calls 'tour player fundamentals' – and fitness, the huge sums of money in the game has also had an effect. As well as making multimillionaires of the top players, it has also kept more journeymen going, the occasional big pay day meaning they can keep searching for the magic formula, whereas before they would have had to give up and get a proper job.

So there may be more players who can be competitive, but Ken Brown, the former Ryder Cup player turned commentator, argues the game is missing something. 'To my mind it is a shame that golf has been so detoxed of everything,' he said. 'Today the fairways are always pristine and the greens like billiard tables, the bunkers are perfect, but actually that is not what golf is all about – it was about getting from that tee to that hole. Now, if it was scruffy all the way then it was the same for everybody. It's not about fairness. It's the same golf but completely different. You had to be a lot more adaptable before. Now the courses are very predictable, the requirements are very predictable. There are fewer skills to be good at.'

If there are fewer skills to be good at, you can spend more time perfecting the ones you need. Inevitably, standards rise, but if players are not required to be as adaptable, is it a less interesting game to watch? 'Tournament golf,' Pat Ward-Thomas wrote 30 years ago, 'could well become an exhibition of technical efficiency by a host of somewhat faceless young men and the age of enduring heroes will have vanished. There would be a fresh one every week.' To some extent, if you are talking about tour golf, then this prediction has come true. It is harder for the great players to separate themselves from the rest. But predictions that there will never again be any dominant players, while perhaps understandable, I believe will prove groundless. Didn't we just have Tiger Woods? Oh, yes, but we'll not see the like of him again. Oh, no?

We have been here before. Hutchinson wrote:

> Golfers may come and golfers may go, but it is very much open to doubt whether any golfer will be quite the idol of the day as Young Tom was during his brilliant career, and certainly no golfer since, probably not even Harry Vardon, has shown yet the decided superiority over all rivals that he was called upon to meet as did the pride of St. Andrews.

Well, Vardon was only just getting going when Hutchinson wrote that. Then came Jones, then Hogan, and Nicklaus, and Woods. Maybe Rory McIlroy will be next, or maybe his US Open victory will prove just a glorious one-off. Either way, it will be fun to find out.

For while there are a few championships each year that players want to win more than the week-to-week fare, when the test is at its sternest and where players are inspired by the grandest of occasions to perform better than they have ever have before, as Darren Clarke did at Sandwich in 2011, then there will always be golfers who reveal themselves as the greatest of them all.

But who is the greatest *ever* golfer? And is it even a sensible thing to try and determine? Jack Nicklaus wrote in *My Story*:

What Bob Jones did, just as Harry Vardon before him and Ben Hogan after him, was to become the best golfer of his time. That's all any man can do, and it is what I have been trying to do all through my career. If when my playing days are finally over I am judged to have succeeded, that will do just fine for an epitaph.

Nicklaus was certainly the best golfer of his time, and arguably for a longer time than anyone else was the best golfer of *their* time.

But he is right in saying that you can only compare how players related to the players they faced. Comparing directly, in absolute terms, men and women, amateurs and professionals, over a century and a half, with changing conditions of courses and equipment and ever-increasing depth of competition, is unhelpful and irrelevant. In any sport where measurements are taken, standards are improving – for instance, times for running and swimming and cycling are getting lower, and distances for throwing or jumping are getting higher.

No-one disputes that technically golfers are getting better. But golf is a game of 'situation'. It is about how to handle this shot, with this club, on this course, against this opponent. That has not changed and never will. It is the reason character is tested as much as technique and the reason why the great champions of the past cannot just be dismissed as inferior to more modern players. It is also one of the reasons why this book does not just contain the top 100 from today's world ranking.

Ranking players in golf has a long tradition, and for much of the 20th century the money list of the PGA Tour sufficed. In the 1980s, a world ranking was developed, but sadly it cannot be backdated to cover the whole period we are considering. Yet no systematic ranking, however sophisticated, could take into account all the variables we are looking at. In the *History of the PGA Tour*, a points table rated players from 1916 to 1988. Sam Snead, still the greatest winner on the circuit, came out top, Nicklaus was second, Arnold Palmer third and Ben Hogan fourth. But take a look at the table for 1953. Top of the list was Doug Ford; in 14th place was Hogan, who hardly played that year but still won four times, three of them majors. In golfing terms, Hogan owns 1953 the same way Bobby Jones owns 1930.

In any case, any systematic approach is only as good as the original assumptions on which it is based – so let's not pretend this is anything other than a completely subjective debate in which the fun is in putting forward an opinion to be disagreed with.

Perhaps we could imagine a championship to end all championships. Dan Jenkins once wrote up such a mythical showdown in *Golf Digest* in the same brilliant style as his major championship reports. He had Sam Snead always taking a triple bogey at the last and, if memory serves, Ben Hogan was his ultimate champion. Attempting to rewrite Jenkins would be sacrilege, but the device might allow us to examine some of the pairings in the final round of a championship in which these particular 100 great golfers were playing. In a show of youthful exuberance perhaps Sergio Garcia and Rory McIlroy would be in the thick of it in the early stages. Greg Norman and Ernie Els might contest the first-round lead. Hopefully, the course would allow the pairing of Henry Cotton and Catherine Lacoste to compare their skills with a one-iron. Joe Carr and Freddie Tait would be all over the place but there would be plenty of spectators to help them find their more wayward efforts.

But, as the championship wore on, there would surely be certain names jostling at the top of the leaderboard: Walter Hagen, Byron Nelson, Sam Snead, Gary Player, Gene Sarazen, Tom Watson, Sir Nick Faldo, Annika Sörenstam, Yani Tseng and, doubtless causing merry hell, Babe Zaharias. But as the final round begins, who might be in the final few pairings? Here are the ten players who might make up the last five groups to tee off:

YOUNG TOM MORRIS · HARRY VARDON

Two early idols of the game in a welcome return to competition. They make a contrasting pair. Morris a dasher, Vardon relentlessly accurate, which only adds more fascination to a contest that has been dreamt about for more than a century.

JOYCE WETHERED · MICKEY WRIGHT

The two greatest ever women players. Jones said he had never been as outclassed as he was when playing with Wethered – he might have been modest but he was not prone to exaggeration. Wright dominated her era like a cross between Hogan and Nicklaus. Can they be separated? The heart says Wethered, the head Wright.

SEVERIANO BALLESTEROS · ARNOLD PALMER

This might just be the most popular two-ball of them all. No need to hype this charismatic duo. The fairways would be packed on either side and, given their attacking and scrambling styles, there would be plenty of chances to get up-close-and-personal. They met at Wentworth in 1983 in the first round of the World Match Play. Palmer was giving away 28 years to a man in his prime but the Spaniard still had to hole a long, running chip at the last for an eagle to halve the match before winning at the third extra hole. Time for a rematch.

TIGER WOODS · BEN HOGAN

The identity of the top four should not surprise. Just trailing the final two are Woods and Hogan. Tiger still has time to force a reassessment but at present he just sneaks into third on the basis of his 14 major victories compared to Hogan's nine. They might make an unlikely pairing but what they have in common is an incredible work ethic. At least, Woods certainly did little else but practise early in his career before injuries forced him to cut back and other things in life became a distraction. Woods might have been the more naturally talented, since it took Hogan until he was the age Tiger is now before finding his prime, but Woods spent two years remodelling his game under Butch Harmon before equalling Hogan's feat from 1953 of winning three majors in a row in 2000. Of course, he added the Masters in 2001 to become the first and only man to hold all four professional majors at the same time. It was his Jones moment, albeit not a calendar-year Grand Slam, but whether he has the longevity to overtake Nicklaus's 18 majors will depend on whether he can remain free from injury.

BOBBY JONES · JACK NICKLAUS

In truth, still the only two contenders for the greatest ever golfer. Either will do perfectly. At different times, both men were named Golfer of the Century well before the end of the 20th century. The weight of opinion today tends towards Nicklaus. In 2000 *Golf Digest* put him top of their list of the 50 greatest players of all time. Hogan was second, Snead third and Jones fourth. *Golf* magazine in 2009 had Nicklaus first, Woods second, Jones third and Hogan fourth. Nicklaus is the game's greatest professional, dominant for two decades but essentially a leading figure in golf his whole life. He won 18 professional majors and two US Amateurs, a record no one has come close to matching. Jones is the game's greatest amateur, a man who scaled its heights and then retired at the age of 28. He did not compete as long as Nicklaus, but he was utterly triumphant when he did. Even if you take out his amateur successes, in 15 appearances in the US Open and the Open Championship, he was the winner or runner-up 11 times.

One quality Jones possessed perhaps even more than Nicklaus, who was better at it than all his direct competitors, was the ability to rise to the challenge of the biggest occasion seemingly on demand. Nicklaus wrote, in a series of articles about the qualities required by a perfect champion, in the *Daily Telegraph* in 2006:

> Perhaps the truest test of a player is whether you can rise to the greatest of occasions. When you are on the course you have to be able to concentrate at the right times and think clearly at the right times. But it starts even before you get to an event. You have to be able to take your game and bring it up for the occasion. Tiger has shown he can do this by winning all four majors in a row but you have to go back to Bobby Jones. He was the ultimate big occasion player. He won the original grand slam – the Opens and Amateurs of the US and Britain – in 1930 but he didn't play very much. Even in 1930, his great year, he only played in six events and won five of them. That's pretty amazing.

While I am not implying that Nicklaus thinks Jones is the greatest ever player, the quality that he identifies is one that I think is important, is most important, in assessing the greatest of the greats. It may be a romantic notion, but the legend of Jones will do for me.

There are plenty of golf writers now filing for the *Celestial Times* who would agree. Henry Longhurst said: 'Jones was probably the greatest and certainly the best-loved golfer of them all.' Charles Price, who saw all the greats of the 20th century, bar Vardon and Woods, wrote:

Bob Jones was the greatest championship golfer in the history of the game, amateur or pro, and I mean championship golfer, not a tournament player. Some men who played golf after Jones hit the ball further, some maybe straighter. Certainly, many had scored lower. A lot of them won way more tournaments and one of them, Jack Nicklaus, more championships. But nobody ever played golf like Bobby Jones.

Sidney L. Matthew is a present-day biographer of Jones and wrote:

Jones had the respect of his peers and all others not because he was the best sportsman. Rather, Jones was the most able man anyone has ever seen. He was the truest-hearted, most just, and noblest of all the golfers who ever lived. He represents the summation of all the qualities that command our willing subordination. Which is why Robert Tyre Jones is and will forever remain ... the Emperor.

But other opinions are available, and a few are provided below to further the discussion. Many more might have been added but that would make for another book. Whether you are talking about the 100 Greatest Ever Golfers or trying to narrow it down to the greatest of the great, it is a debate that is both timeless and endless, which makes for all the more fun during those long hours at the 19th hole.

'Hogan was the greatest shot-maker who ever lived. He won tournaments without being able to putt real good like these guys today. He played on uneven courses, uneven greens and strong competition with Sam Snead, Byron Nelson, Jimmy Demaret and all those guys.

He concentrated on winning majors, especially the US Open. I say he won five – I count the wartime one, as did he – they issued him a medal just like the other four. He won more majors over a shorter period of time than anybody. I still say Nicklaus was the greatest winner but Hogan was the greatest shot-maker.'

Dan Jenkins, golf writer

'It has to be Jack Nicklaus. I would caveat that, Lee Trevino was not very far behind of those that I have seen play. I'm talking about a career as well. Tiger Woods played the best golf that has ever been played for a period but as things stand Jack Nicklaus is the greatest player over a career. It's everything about him, the record he created and how he conducted himself, ruthless competitor, tremendous player, no silly rickets, win, lose or draw.'

Ken Brown, Ryder Cup player

'Still Jack, because of the 18 majors. But the way Tiger has got his 14, he's hit shots most of us couldn't dream of, let alone hit. But Jack was my inspiration, he's the reason I am here.'

Sir Nick Faldo

'Tiger Woods. Took over from Jack Nicklaus as the player who dominated the game in a period when the game had moved on into an athletic sport. When Nicklaus dominated it, it was not such an athletic sport. Nicklaus had the great strength of mind, the calmness, he had the great mental capacity. What Tiger brought were all the strengths of Jack plus the athleticism. The absolute common desire between the both was to dominate the game but one did it with brute strength, Nicklaus could dominate the field with brute power, and Tiger took it up a gear by doing it with athletic power.'

Denis Pugh, coach

'Tiger Woods, hands down. Mentally, physically, playability-wise, not just the 14 majors but you add in the 15 World Golf Championships which are played against major fields then you have 29 events, that is extraordinary in this era. Extraordinary.'

Colin Montgomerie

ACKNOWLEDGEMENTS

This book would not have been possible without golfers who have been the greatest ever. The greatest, however, would not exist with there being great golfers, and very good golfers, and good ones, and not so good ones ... and even those of us who may only be termed 'hackers'. We all have our place in the pyramid.

But if there is one golfer who could be singled out it is the late Severiano Ballesteros. There are people of a certain age, particularly British males, who might not now be working in golf without the inspiration of the magical Spaniard who so utterly captured our imaginations. He invited us to love golf; we accepted willingly.

Seve's major-winning days were behind him when I started working as a golf writer. But the first European Tour event on which I reported for *Golf Weekly*, the PGA Championship in 1991, was won by Ballesteros. On the 17th hole, he was in amongst the gallery, having almost found another fairway, when he was distracted by someone behind him. He whipped round, glaring at the miscreant and asked: 'You nervooos?' Then came that smile. 'It's ok, me nervooos, too.' At the winner's press conference afterwards, it was impossible not to be completely awestruck. Yet, looking around at all the hardened hacks who had covered Seve his entire career, they were all equally spellbound.

As Seve's form waned, he found himself trying to explain why he had missed the cut, not why he had won. In Spain, where understanding of the sport was limited at the time, he would get frustrated with the press. But he always had words for the British writers who were present. It was his way of repaying them for following him over his entire career and, by extension, the British golfing public with whom he always felt the closest connection.

At the Ryder Cup in 1995, he played the most extraordinary golf for nine holes in the lead singles against Tom Lehman. The American seemed to find every fairway and every green. He never saw Seve, who was everywhere but on the fairways and the greens. Lehman should have been winning easily but he turned only one-up. Everyone on the property knew this was absurd and his fighting spirit helped inspire a European comeback to take victory that night.

But the most extraordinary thing I ever saw on a golf course came in the European Masters at Crans-sur-Sierre in 1993. Ballesteros was on the 18th hole having played the previous four holes in eagle-bogey-birdie-birdie. He was on a charge and it was thrilling, but now he missed the fairway on the right after a wild slice. Believing he needed one more birdie to have a chance to win, Seve looked at the shot he faced. His ball was six feet from a six-foot high wall. He was under the branches of a couple of trees. There was no way he could advance his ball to the green, except for the tiniest of gaps that only he saw. His caddie, Billy Foster, pleaded with his man to chip out sideways. 'Seve,' he said, 'for the last time, it's impossible.'

'I don't know why you think it is impossible?' came the indignant reply. 'I think it is possible. I can get it on the green. It's a big risk but it is possible.'

Foster could not watch. No one could, except it was a good idea seeing how the ball might rebound anywhere from the wall. 'He might kill himself,' a colleague said. Seve swung and the ball did exactly what he wanted it to do, going over the water but under the tree branches, over a swimming pool, the corner of a hospitality tent, a tree and a bunker. Not quite exactly. The ball was not on the green but it was just in front of it. He was 18 yards from the hole and had to go over the corner of another bunker but with the same pitching wedge with which he had hit the previous miraculous shot, he chipped in. The noise was deafening in the Alps. Seve punched the air and kept on punching. Foster sank to his knees and bowed before his master.

Ballesteros ended up one short of the winner Barry Lane. When asked later why he did not play backwards to the fairway, as Foster had demanded, Seve said: 'I wanted to make three. I was looking to win. I am always looking to go forwards, not backwards. I make more miracle shots than anyone else because I try harder than anyone else and take more risks.' Later he got a big grin on his face and added: 'If I play to the fairway it is not news. This is news. This is a story.'

It is no good the game's greatest players providing great stories if there is no one around to tell them. The second debt this book owes is to the great golf writers of the past who have chronicled the game's great players and great moments. Being sidetracked and led astray by the writings of greats from Bernard Darwin to Dan Jenkins while researching this book was time-consuming, inevitable and thoroughly enjoyable. Their gems provided the thread to follow on the winding trail from Allan Robertson to Rory McIlroy.

Among those quoted most often are:

Horace Hutchinson, twice Amateur champion and early golfing historian

Harold Hilton, twice Open champion and prolific golf writer and editor

Bernard Darwin, grandson of Charles; 1922 Walker Cup player, 1934 R&A captain, golf correspondent of *The Times* and peerless golfing author

Herb Warren Wind, writer for *Sports Illustrated* and *The New Yorker*, after whom the USGA's annual book award is named

Charles Price, American golf writer and author, whose *A Golf Story* is a superb telling of the life of Bobby Jones and the history of the Masters

Pat Ward-Thomas, golf correspondent of the *Guardian* and columnist for *Country Life*

Henry Longhurst, columnist for the *Sunday Times* and television commentator

Peter Ryde, golf correspondent of *The Times* and co-editor with Donald Steel of the *Shell International Encyclopedia of Golf*

Peter Dobereiner, golf correspondent of the *Observer* and the *Guardian*, and columnist for *Golf Digest* and *Golf World* (UK)

Robert Sommers, author and longtime historian for the United States Golf Association

David Davies, golf correspondent of the *Guardian*

Peter Alliss, Ryder Cup player turned television commentator and golf writer

Donald Steel, sometime golf correspondent of the *Sunday Telegraph* and golf course architect

Dan Jenkins, writer for *Sports Illustrated* and *Golf Digest*, and one of golf's funniest authors

Liz Kahn, British freelance golf writer who interviewed all the great American women players for her history of the Ladies Professional Golf Association

Lewine Mair, former golf correspondent of the *Daily Telegraph*

To all my current golf writing colleagues who have offered advice, opinions, guidance and encouragement, I am truly grateful, as ever. Thanks are due also for the sterling efforts of Charles Briscoe-Knight and Dale Concannon in providing most of the images for this book, as well as Marlene Streit and Karen Hewson, Director of the Canadian Golf Museum. No thanks is too great, nor praise too high, for all those at Elliott & Thompson who have brought this book into being, especially Lorne Forsyth, Alastair Graham, Olivia Bays and Nick Sidwell.

BIBLIOGRAPHY

Peter Alliss, *Peter Alliss' 100 Greatest Golfers*, Queen Anne Press, 1989; *Peter Alliss' Golf Heroes*, Virgin Books, 2003

Al Barkow, *The History of the PGA Tour*, Doubleday, 1989

Ted Barrett and Michael Hobbs, *The Ultimate Encyclopedia of Golf*, Carlton Books, 1995

John Behrend, Peter N. Lewis, Keith Mackie, Champions & Guardians, *Royal & Ancient Golf Club of St. Andrews*, 2001

Cal Brown and Robert Sommers, *Great Shots*, Anaya Publishers, 1989

Tom Callahan, *In Search of Tiger*, Mainstream, 2004; *His Father's Son*, Mainstream, 2011

Bernard Darwin, *Golf*, Flagstick Books, 1999, reprint from 1954

David and Patricia Davies, *Beyond the Fairways*, CollinsWillow, 1999

Laura Davies, with Lewine Mair, *Naturally...*, Bloomsbury, 1996

Peter Dobereiner, *Dobereiner on Golf*, Aurum Press, 1998

Alun Evans, *The Golf Majors*, A&C Black, 2002

Mark Frost, *The Greatest Game Ever Played*, Sphere, 2003; *The Grand Slam*, Time Warner, 2004

Harold Hilton and Garden G. Smith, editors, *The Royal & Ancient Game of Golf*, London and Counties Press Association, 1912

Michael Hobbs, editor, *The Golfer's Companion*, Queen Anne Press, 1988

Malcolm Gladwell, *Outliers*, Penguin, 2009; *Blink*, Back Bay Books, 2007

John Jacobs, *50 Years of Golfing Wisdom*, CollinsWillow, 2005

Colin Jarman, *The Ryder Cup*, Contemporary Books, 1999

Dan Jenkins, *Jenkins at the Majors*, Anchor Books, 2010

David Joy, *St. Andrews and the Open Championship*, Sleeping Bear Press, 1999

Liz Kahn, *The LPGA: The History of the Ladies Professional Golf Association*, AA Publishing, 1996

Elliott Kalb, *Who's Better, Who's Best in Golf*, McGraw-Hill, 2005

Renton Laidlaw, editor, *Golfer's Handbook*, Macmillan, various editions

David Mackintosh, editor, *Golf's Greatest Eighteen*, Contemporary Books, 2003

Michael McDonnell, editor, *Classic Golf Quotes*, Robson Books, 2004

Alec Morrison, editor, *The Impossible Art of Golf*, Oxford University Press, 1994

Francis Murray, *The Open*, Pavilion, 2000

Steve Newell, *A History of Golf*, Green Umbrella for Marks & Spencer, 2003; *The Golf Book*, Dorling Kindersley, 2008

Bev Norwood, editor, *The Open Championship*, Aurum Press, various editions

Chris Plumridge, editor, *The Essential Henry Longhurst*, Pan Books, 1990; *The Challenge of Golf*, St. Michael, 1988

Charles Price, *A Golf Story*, Aurum Press, 2001 (1986)

Bud Shrake, *The Best of Harvey Penick*, CollinsWillow, 1997

Gordon G. Simmonds, *The Walker Cup*, Granta, 2000

Calvin H Sinnette, *Forbidden Fairways*, Sleeping Bear Press, 1998

Robert Sommers, *The US Open*, Oxford University Press, 1996; *Golf Anecdotes*, Oxford University Press, 2004

Donald Steel and Peter Ryde, editors, *Shell International Encyclopedia of Golf*, Ebury Press, 1975

Matthew Syed, *Bounce: How Champions are Made*, Fourth Estate, 2010

Basil Ashton Tinkler, *Joyce Wethered: The Great Lady of Golf*, Tempus, 2004

Pat Ward-Thomas, *Not Only Golf*, Hodder and Stoughton, 1981

Michael Williams, *The Official History of the Ryder Cup*, Stanley Paul, 1989

INDEX BY GOLFER